The Essence of Change

DATE			

BAKER & TAYLOR

The Essence of Management Series

Published titles

The Essence of Total Quality Management
The Essence of Strategic Management
The Essence of International Money
The Essence of Management Accounting
The Essence of Financial Accounting
The Essence of Marketing Research
The Essence of Information Systems
The Essence of Personal Microcomputing
The Essence of Successful Staff Selection
The Essence of Effective Communication
The Essence of Statistics for Business
The Essence of Business Taxation
The Essence of the Economy
The Essence of Mathematics for Business
The Essence of Organizational Behaviour
The Essence of Small Business
The Essence of Business Economics
The Essence of Operations Management
The Essence of Services Marketing
The Essence of International Business
The Essence of Marketing

Forthcoming titles

The Essence of Public Relations
The Essence of Managing People
The Essence of Financial Management
The Essence of Business Law
The Essence of International Marketing
The Essence of Women in Management
The Essence of Mergers and Acquisitions
The Essence of Industrial Relations and Personnel Management
The Essence of Influencing Skills
The Essence of Services Management
The Essence of Industrial Marketing
The Essence of Venture Capital and New Ventures

The Essence of Change

Liz Clarke

Prentice Hall

New York   London   Toronto   Sydney   Tokyo   Singapore

First published 1994 by
Prentice Hall International (UK) Ltd
Campus 400, Maylands Avenue
Hemel Hempstead
Hertfordshire, HP2 7EZ
A division of
Simon & Schuster International Group

Typeset in 10/12 pt Palatino
by Keyset Composition, Colchester

Printed and bound in Great Britain by
BPC Wheatons Ltd, Exeter

Library of Congress Cataloging-in-Publication Data

Clarke, Liz
    The essence of change / Liz Clarke.
        p.   cm. — (The Essence of management series)
    Includes bibliographical references and index.
    ISBN 0–13–030222–8
    1. Organizational change—Management.   I. Title.   II. Series.
HD58.8.C525 1994
658.4′06—dc20   93–36651
                                                                      CIP

British Library Cataloguing in Publication Data

A catalogue record for this book is available from
the British Library

ISBN 0–13–030222–8

---

1 2 3 4 5   98 97 96 95 94

Contents

Foreword

Despite all the downsizing, decentralization and delayering that went on in the 1980s, I know few organizations that couldn't double their performance with a fundamental business rethink.

Change isn't a one-off event, to be followed by 'business as usual' and better-than-last-year planning paradigms. Change has to be built into the very fibre of the enterprise – relearning new versions of the entire business process monthly, even weekly.

The CEO's annual satellite broadcast and one-week management event won't hack it. The era of the 'spread-sheet' organization is close, where a change in one cell propagates through the entire nervous system hitting the parts which need to know. A torrent of new computing and communications technology is about to transform how work is done – demanding powerful new roadmaps for the complete workforce. The lead-times for change are long, the solution is to start early – get ahead of the power curve, treat internal communications as the marketing challenge of your life – because it is.

Be unreasonable. Why not 20 per cent performance improvement every year? Why not do it in one year instead of three? Why can't I run my business at three times the industry average of sales per employee? Why? Why? Why?

Burrow down into the organization to find the young managers who don't yet know what's impossible. Give them the tools to do it. Galvanize their natural intellectual and emotional energy. You'll never find out what's going on stuck in headquarters – go find out, inside – and out with customers.

Don't tolerate yesterday's men around you – the good old boys who administer the culture that's there to stop you changing anything.

Build your vision, test it, communicate it and stick with it. If your company has to move at 100 mph, you will have plenty of people around from the Board down telling you it will blow up or topple over. Ignore them. But don't ignore the role that information and information systems can play, and don't think that innovation is something that only goes on in R&D – give people the right information and they can't help but innovate.

ICL is one of the corporate examples explored in this book. It is ten years since ICL's transformation gained such visibility in the change management world – much more impressive in my view is the continuous change that has occurred since, keeping the company ahead of the industry pitfalls – allowing it to prosper while hundreds of thousands lost their jobs elsewhere. So in reading this excellent book, look for the clues that lead to continuous performance improvement, not just a one-off blitz.

Robb Wilmot
Chairman, OASIS Group plc

Introduction

This book was prompted by my work as a consultant in the 1980s and early 1990s, with companies that were trying to transform their organizations in order to cope with dramatic market and environmental change. Above the usual noises of organizational discontent were appearing new rumblings with a distinctly different tenor, all about the fear, pain and excitement of change.

These organizational discoveries coincided with a period of personal change where I found myself struggling with the issues of challenging old assumptions, letting go and moving on. It seemed to me that the journeys of personal and organizational change are much the same and that learnings in one arena can enrich the other. I hope that by sharing the experiences of others you will be able to embrace the journey of change rather than facing it with fear.

The Essence of Change is about how to make change happen, building corporate experiences of successful and unsuccessful change and providing practical insight into the process of change. The sad fact is that even the most powerful leaders are highly dependent on the capacity of the organization and the people they lead to produce the changes they require. It is only by understanding *how* people work within organizations that we can create sustainable change.

This book is a practitioner's guide on how to create, sustain and manage change through individuals and organizational teams. The chapters are developed as a coherent philosophy of change, which is summarized in Figure I.1. Equally you can dip into particular chapters which touch on your key concerns.

Good luck on your personal and organizational journey of change!

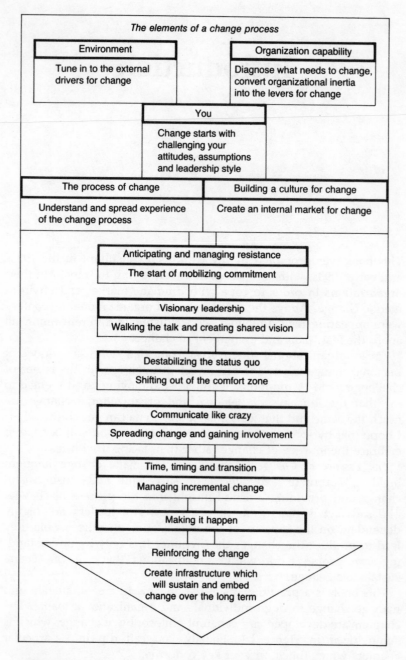

Figure I.1 How to create, manage and sustain business change

With grateful thanks to the friends, colleagues and organizations without whom there would be no book. In particular: Dr Hans Joerg Frank from whom it all sprang and to whom the book is dedicated; Pat Bundy for her usual good-humoured energy in converting illegible scribble into manuscript; Colin Barrow for aggressive encouragement to get ideas on paper; Gilly Rigo-Andrews and Liz Eckford, fellow passengers on the journey; Lorraine Bateman for powerful moments of illumination; Barrie Haigh for letting me take his name in vain; to the memory of Dr Pat Terry for opening my eyes to the magic of organizations; and Mike Watson for sharing with me his vision of the future.

1

Tune in to the external environment

1.1 Mapping a new future

The last decade has brought with it a time of totally unprecedented change. In every direction businesses are in turmoil, from computing to financial services, from telecommunications to health care. Change is an accelerating constant and yet there is a fundamental dilemma. People need time to get used to change, but there isn't any time any more. The pace of change is now so fast that businesses face constant market change and must respond very rapidly if they are to survive. Many don't make it. Evidence suggests that the average corporate lifespan is down to forty years and, like product lifecycles, may be shrinking because of an inability to change and adapt fast enough. For this reason managing change has now become a crucial part of competitive edge.

The need for organizations to change is far more clearly recognized now than a few years ago when the question 'Why change?' was paramount. Few people nowadays would argue with the premiss 'change or die'. Mastering change is increasingly part of every manager's job. Managers who are good at creating sustainable change have an extensive understanding of the environment surrounding the business, where the main threats and opportunities lie. As Figure I.1 indicates, the start point lies in tuning into and constantly monitoring and scanning these external drivers for change. Unless we link organization change with changing market realities we are merely tinkering with cosmetic results, lurching from crisis to crisis, restructuring *ad infinitum*.

1

Figure 1.1 Scanning the business environment

This chapter tells you how to scan your business environment and pick up the signals for change which will stop you from being boiled alive. It also enables you to decide where your business is on a growth curve and therefore what challenges to prepare yourself for. As Figure 1.1 illustrates, although it will become important later to diagnose organizational capability, strengths and weakness, the start point for change is not organizational navel-gazing, rather it is looking outward to the major 'stakeholders' in the business and identifying what is changing and how it will impact on you. It means identifying the few important trends and issues to which your organization is particularly vulnerable. Perhaps the most famous example is Shell, who anticipated the oil crisis of the early 1970s, enabling it to respond more effectively than its competitors when the unthinkable actually happened. Not only are the separate elements of the environment, such as the marketplace, changing dramatically, but the 'membrane' between the organization and its environment is becoming much more permeable as, for example, businesses contract out services. Nor do the separate aspects of the environment stay separate. Those who were customers become competitors, suppliers become partners, competitors become joint ventures, while employees can become marketplace, suppliers or competitors!

Understanding change and staying alive means adapting to and influencing the specific business environment within which you operate. This is where the rules of engagement are defined. This means asking the question: 'What is happening out there and how do we need to adapt?' The story of Hewlett Packard reacting to changed circumstances indicates the size of the challenge.

Hewlett Packard: from dinosaur to adaptive paragon

The computer industry has experienced an extraordinarily dynamic rate of change. For example, between 1987 and 1992, both the number of computers in use and the memory of each has multiplied a thousand-fold. Some of the mighty pioneers of the industry such as IBM and even some of the sexy newcomers like Compaq have suffered through their failure to keep up with drastic technology and market change. In 1990 it looked as though Hewlett Packard might be among their number. The *Wall Street Journal* had described the company as 'a torpid dinosaur amongst fleet footed little predators'. Since then however, the company has changed tack. It has recognized and even anticipated profound changes in the distribution channels through which competitors sell. Hewlett Packard used to sell around a dozen 'state of the art' measuring devices each month to highly sophisticated specialists. Now it produces 125,000 laser jets a week and distributes to mail order warehouses all over the world. It has become 'an adaptive paragon'.

Hewlett Packard believe that it is only by anticipating what will be needed some day in the future and ensuring that when that day comes the product is in place, that they give themselves a chance of survival. Bill Hewlett, at 78 still active in the business, gives some clues about the secret of their success:

- 'Above all treat change as inevitable, don't try to resist it.'
- 'Always be ready to take a 45 degree turn when you see a direction that is new and promising.'

The Hewlett Packard story contrasts strikingly with how IBM

handled similarly drastic changes in its marketplace. Managing change is always easy with hindsight but it is extraordinary that IBM managed to ignore the writing on the wall for so long. Rumblings of change had been around since the mid-1980s but even in 1992 *The Economist* could portray Mr John Akers, then at the helm, as a construction manager hard hat on head poised in his chair, mallet in hand facing the direction of the supposed challenge while an enormous demolition ball swings down from behind him to knock him into oblivion!

Part of the problem for IBM was that it had been so huge and successful for so long that it couldn't or wouldn't believe that the world and the rules were changing. Technology meant that by the 1990s the mainframe was about as relevant to business as the abacus: but IBM's strategy and strengths were in mainframes. Customer preferences were changing, because they had new options which meant that they didn't have to be tied in to IBM-compatible systems and once the door was opened, they ran. Similarly, IBM drastically underestimated the competition – Microsoft in particular.

The lessons for the rest of us are powerful. If it can happen to IBM it can happen to anyone; the cost of complacency comes high. We can adopt the Hewlett Packard rather than the IBM approach by constantly recognizing and even anticipating new challenges. This means putting in place processes to get and keep close to the customers. It means customer panels, getting senior management out into the field, creating channels for articulating and diagnosing customer problems. More and more, the new world is too complex to be read by one man at the top, so tuning into the external environment is a job not only for senior management, but for everyone. It must be part of an educational process which encourages all managers to anticipate new worlds.

Very often senior managers will hold workshops for themselves to scan the environment and identify new business and customer trends. This is excellent; however, they often miss a trick. Too frequently they then present their outcomes as a *fait accompli* to the next level down, who are asked to translate them into action. This causes resentment, minimal commitment and lack of real 'gut'-level understanding of how the marketplace is shifting. Why not allow each level of management and staff to reinvent the wheel, to scan the environment themselves? This is a great source of 'buy-in' to change.

The technique of 'scenario planning', invented by Herman Kahn, is a great way of taking the blinkers off, by involving people in identifying external trends and anticipating how they may impact on the business. The power of 'what-ifing' and creating a world of 'virtual reality' is not that of crystal ball gazing, for the pace of change is so great that what is anticipated is unlikely to be what actually happens, the power of the technique lies in creating mental muscle and flexibility, like a tennis player limbering up on the base line so that he is prepared for the ball from whatever direction it may come.

For the first time ever, looking at the past doesn't help us predict the future. We have to chart new futures as we go. The management map is being transformed for good, yet the management map is itself only part of the 'world map' of change. The sheer scale of the changes which have overtaken us in the late twentieth century is powerfully illustrated by even the most cursory glance at recent events in the political, social, market, technological and environmental arenas.

1.1.1 Changes in the political map

Roll up your map of Europe! Tidal waves of change have been crashing across Central Europe and the Soviet Union. Who would have predicted the sudden domino effect as change swept across Eastern Europe bringing the collapse of the Berlin Wall, the death of the USSR, the emergence of Islam? Changes have gone beyond the bounds of ordinary politics, our leaders find it difficult to address them, they simply transcend normal categories of thought. What is the future of a united Europe? What will be the impact of German reunification on world history? Where will the next challenge come from?

1.1.2 Changes in the social map

Recent census statistics demonstrate how astonishingly the face of family life in Britain is changing:

- The average household size is down to 2.47 people.
- The proportion of people living on their own is heading up to nearly 30 per cent nationally.
- Only a quarter of households now consist of a married couple and their children.
- Only 15 per cent of children go to church (compared to 50 per cent in the 1950s).

- Of the new jobs created since 1970, 90 per cent have been taken by women.
- In the 1990s the Department of Employment expects eight or more out of every ten new jobs to go to women.

1.1.3   Globalization of markets

Domestic markets no longer mean domestic competition. Two decades ago, import of goods and services was equivalent to just 5.4 per cent of the United States' GNP. By the start of the 1990s that had risen to 13 per cent. There has been a huge rise in import-penetration in the major economies. The only stage to play on is the world stage.

In their book *Managing Across Borders* Christopher Bartlett of Harvard Business School and Sumantra Ghoshal of Insead identify four types of 'world' company: global, international, multinational and their ideal, the transnational company, which thinks globally but acts locally as conditions dictate. The odds are that tomorrow's bosses will have to be able to manage decentralized organizations which are a kaleidoscope of different cultures, different customer preferences and different product strategies.

1.1.4   Acceleration of technology change

Product and technology cycles are shrinking at a terrifying rate, especially in Japan. The average model life of a European car in 1991 was 12 years, a Japanese car 4½ years and falling. New product technology is shortening lifecycles, new computer and telecommunications technologies are reducing physical distances which act as a barrier between people and countries and creating new systems and infrastructures.

1.1.5   Going green

Environmental pressures for change are not a fad. Businesses ignore them at their peril. One recent survey suggested that 50 per cent of French and 80 per cent of West German consumers choose environmentally friendly goods when shopping in supermarkets.

To keep pace with such changes in almost every aspect of their environment, businesses are being forced to discard their old assumptions. The traditional vertical, functional hierarchy has gone for good, businesses are delayering, becoming smaller and flatter.

Using Charles Handy's 'shamrock' principle (1990), businesses are realizing that they only need a small 'core' of full-time workers and that much of the rest can be subcontracted out to part-timers and temporary labour. Those clear boundaries between the business and its external environment are breaking down as competitors become partners in joint ventures, and suppliers become part of the design process.

Change is being driven by new technology, by new markets and customer preferences, by political and governmental pressures, by social expectations. The world is fluid, complex, unsettled and unsettling and it is unlikely to get less so. Our old reassurances have gone: 'Why don't top management get it right and then we can stop changing?' is a cry in the wilderness. At a recent management conference one manager, in a state of blind optimism, commented on a huge internal reorganization: 'I really think this is the last big one.' This was greeted by gales of laughter from his management colleagues. Change is a constant process, there is no arrival point. Longed-for periods of stability seem to have evaporated. The complexity is such that no one person can predict the lie of the land. There are few blueprints for the future in the boardrooms of major businesses.

Herman Miller: no arrival point

Herman Miller is a vast American company manufacturing prestige office furniture and famous for its 'warm' culture. Mike Knight, Director of Customer Service in Herman Miller UK, talks about changes in the European organization and market strategy:

> There is no arrival point for change, lots of managers don't realize that continuity has gone for good. This exhausts people until you realize it's the norm. There is no going back. We need a state of mind of continuous evolution made possible by a degree of stability in the processes we use.

Herman Miller will need its 'state of mind of continuous evolution' if its European operation is to thrive through the 1990s. In the last few years its market dominance through products such as the famous 'Eames chair' has been severely jolted by massive competitive activity and by the driving down of prices and margins. The new CEO in the United States has reorganized, creating the now familiar flatter structures and emphasizing 'empowerment', management education continues despite cost pressures and the company is

attempting to surface new market opportunities continuously, identifying not only the current concerns of customers but also the
questions they haven't yet asked, which may be signposts to the
future.

1.2   The past doesn't help anymore

Change is the very essence of business growth: it's inevitable and
unavoidable. Strange, then, that we insist on operating on the
misleading assumption that things will stay the same. Unfortunately, what worked in the past won't in the future – a lesson which is
particularly tough to learn for successful businesses which believe in
their own mythology.

It is a disconcerting fact that in business, history counts for very
little. Big companies assume the trappings of permanence, they
erect ostentatious buildings, promote their own history and in
general behave as if they've been around since time began. But
stability is a sham. If customers stop buying even briefly, the
greatest of corporate edifices will begin to crumble. A new rival or a
new technology can rapidly shift the ground under even the most
respected of firms. The *Financial Times*, commenting on ICI's bifurca-
tion plans of 1993, said: 'The demerger is a splendid example of how
a supposedly hidebound management can be rendered nimble by a
sense of threat.' Yet a propensity for continual change has been
described as capitalism's greatest virtue.

The most remarkable thing about our great corporations is not
their longevity but their transience. Of the hundred firms heading
the *Fortune 500* list of top American companies published in 1956,
only twenty-nine could be found in the top 100 by 1992. Within the
space of one working life well over a third of them have been jostled
out of the way by more agile competitors.

Success frequently brings with it a huge investment in past
solutions and the status quo. There is a high probability that past
success actually holds the seeds of future downfall – take the mighty
Lloyds of London trying to weather recent storms.

Lloyds of London

Lloyds of London has been described as 'a garden where the rabbits
were put in charge of the lettuce' (*The Economist*). The Lloyds market
has a 300-year-old history and many time-honoured traditions. It is a

kind of gentlemen's club previously inviolable to external pressures. It has taken a crisis of gigantic proportions to jar Lloyds out of its lethargic conservatism. The catastrophic losses of the late 1980s and early 1990s caused nearly 6,000 out of 32,400 'names' to resign between 1988 and 1991 – a fair indication of customer dissatisfaction. The Lutine bell started to ring for Lloyds, but it was a long time before its warning was heeded. Survival means drastic change in culture and structure. Some of Lloyds' most cherished assumptions, such as 'unlimited liability', have had to be reassessed. The rules of the game have changed.

Whether you are a Lloyds name or not, whether you have had to sell your Lonsdale Belt or not, the lessons in managing change are striking. First, never ignore the rumblings of dissatisfaction from customers; they indicate not only criticism but the opportunity and direction of change. Second, accept that the rules of the game will inescapably change in every business. Don't become a victim of your own success. As the hugely successful Glaxo Group is finding out, the point at which you should open yourself to the possibility of new rules and new behaviours is actually at the point of greatest success, not after things have started to shift dramatically. Third, have some process of external audit not only of your financial 'health' but of your organizational 'health', so that you get a view unbiased by internal politics, of where you are, where you're going and how to get there. You may be too close to read the writing on the wall.

1.3 Predictable cycles of change

Like the seasons, human activities seem to go through predictable cycles of change, whether we're looking at individuals moving through the life passages of youth, maturity, old age and death or whether we're looking at long-wave cycles in the world economy. In Figure 1.2 Kondratiev postulates that all capitalist systems are

First decade:	Deep slump
Second decade:	The upswing starts
Third decade:	New world dawns
Fourth decade:	Doubt sets in
Fifth decade:	The crazy one: fluctuation and setback

Figure 1.2 Kondratiev's long-wave cycles

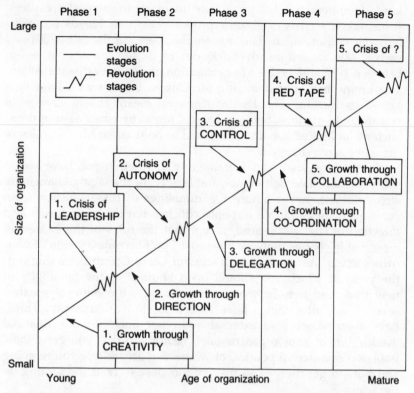

Source: An exhibit from 'Evolution and revolution as organizations grow' by Larry E.
Greiner. Reprinted by permission of the *Harvard Business Review*, July/August 1972

Figure 1.3 The five phases of growth

subject to long-wave cycles, somewhere between 50 and 60 years in
length, and that we are currently trying to break through out of a
fifth decade downturn before presumably hitting the 'deep slump'
which precedes upswing! Kondratiev sees technology as the catalyst
for change. Where in the past it was railways or canals or air travel
which provided the catalyst, he now envisages information technology as the lever which will move us out of one cycle into the
next: 'Plus ça change.'

Similarly, all organizations move through predictable phases of
growth, as described in Greiner's influential model (Figure 1.3). As
the organization gets older and larger it goes through five phases of
development, representing cycles of evolution and revolution.

Greiner provides an insight into the changes in organizational structure, strategy and behaviour that need to be achieved if the business is to move on to the next phase of growth. By implication his research reveals that most firms never learn the lessons, or at least not in time. At best they seem caught in a time-warp, unable to expand beyond a particular size or phase of growth. (Whatever happened to the much vaunted new 'start-ups' in the Cambridge Science Park and how many have grown into large mature businesses?)

The Greiner model outlines the characteristics of each phase of growth and provides a framework to help manage through the crises. Greiner emphasizes that there are no safe havens, for just like a child growing up, all we know is that the next crisis will be different from the last one!

The Greiner model has a lot going for it for any management team that is undergoing change. First of all, it will provide you with a shared language, a common vocabulary for talking about change and spreading experience of the change process. Second, you and your team can use the John Leppard questionnaire to identify where your business is on the growth curve, enabling you to discuss what kind of issues you can anticipate in the future. Third, and perhaps most important, Greiner's framework legitimizes the need for change in terms of different phases of business growth. Inevitably, what worked in the past won't in the future. It's a question of 'appropriateness' or 'fit'; change is not a personal criticism of managers' competence nor an attack on the past. It's interesting that even Greiner's crystal ball couldn't tell him what lay at the end of Phase 5 growth! Perhaps one recycles back to the beginning, as indeed are many large companies who are trying to relearn the lessons of their youth and build back an entrepreneurial culture.

Figure 1.4 outlines some of the differences and dilemmas of each phase of growth and starts to sketch out some of the issues which may lie on the organizational agenda for change and which will be explored more fully in Chapter 2.

Let's look in more detail at how businesses handle the predictable crises of growth. These are:

Phase 1: Crisis of leadership
Phase 2: Crisis of autonomy
Phase 3: Crisis of control
Phase 4: Crisis of red tape
Phase 5: Crisis of ?

	Phase 1 Entrepreneurial	Phase 2 Direction	Phase 3 Delegation	Phase 4 Co-ordination	Phase 5 Collaboration
Structure	• Informal	• Functional • Centralized • Hierarchical • Top-down	• Decentralized • Bottom-up	• Staff functions • Strategic business units (SBUs) • Decentralized • Units merged into product groups	• Matrix-type structure
Systems	• Immediate response to customer feedback	• Standards • Cost centres • Budget • Salary systems	• Profit centres • Bonuses • Management by exception	• Formal planning procedures • Investment centres • Tight expenditure controls	• Simplified and integrated information systems
Styles/people	• Individualistic • Creative • Entrepreneurial • Ownership	• Strong directive	• Full delegation and autonomy	• Watchdog	• Team-oriented • Interpersonal skills at a premium • Innovative • Educational bias
Strengths	• Fun • Market response	• Efficient	• High management motivation	• More efficient allocation of corporate and local resources	• Greater spontaneity • Flexible and behavioural approach
Crisis point	• Crisis of leadership	• Crisis of autonomy	• Crisis of control	• Crisis of red tape	?
Weaknesses	• Founder often temperamentally unsuited to managing • Boss overloaded	• Unsuited to diversity • Cumbersome • Hierarchical • Doesn't grow people	• Top managers lose control as freedom breeds parochial attitudes	• Bureaucratic divisions between line/staff, headquarters/field, etc.	• Psychological saturation

Figure 1.4 The stages of growth

1.3.1 Phase 1: growth through creativity

Business start-ups are typically small and, by definition, young. The founder of the business is at the heart of everything. His vision and leadership style are crucial.

Innovex: the happy hunters (early days)

As the chairman of Innovex, Barrie Haigh, surveyed the management team he had created, he had good reason to congratulate himself. In just a few years he had built up a business to £10 million turnover employing over 300 people and specializing in providing medical representation and marketing services to blue-chip pharmaceutical companies. Let's see how he got there.

Innovex started as a typical Phase 1 owner/founder organization. The founder was a first-rate and enormously energetic entrepreneur whose physical and mental energies were absorbed with the customers. 'Success was down to a very few people, primarily the chairman.' Communication among employees was frequent and informal. Long hours of work were rewarded by an involved, happy atmosphere. The approach to customers was action-oriented and the feedback instant. There was a passionate attempt to avoid politics and a disdain of administration.

All this wonderful, creative, exciting buzz was essential for the company to get off the ground. But therein lies the problem. As the company grew in size and age, more efficiency was needed in managing money and resources, new employees didn't always know what was going on, more people made informal communication more difficult to achieve. The company found itself burdened by unwanted management responsibilities which it reluctantly saw as necessary but didn't regard as fun. Instead of everyone being 'happy hunters', the business needed the 'farmers' of a Phase 2 organization.

Here is how people described their organization as they approached the crisis of leadership:

'We're self-centred rather than customer-centred.'
'We're happy amateurs.'
'We're not businessmen, totally top-line sales driven.'
'We're unplanned and confused.'
'It's organized chaos. You sink or swim.'
'We let ourselves down on detail.'

Of course, the Innovex story didn't stop at the end of Phase 1 'growth through creativity'. Change is continuous. In the late 1980s the business moved out of its quaint offices into a streamlined and prestigious building in Henley. Since then it has acquired new buildings and is about to move again. In 1989 the chairman masterminding Phase 2 growth and already anticipating Phase 3 dilemmas took himself off on a Cranfield business growth programme, restructured the company into profit centres, strengthened the management team and delegated responsibility. He faced the key dilemma of growing a business beyond his own resources and after a time-consuming and difficult search, found an excellent managing director allowing Barrie to back off and let go of operational matters. By mid-1993 Innovex had completed an exceptionally successful takeover of a business with German and American interests and had become both a European force and the largest clinical trials organization in the United Kingdom, employing more than 800 people with a combined turnover of well over £30 million.

Innovex says this is only the start of what they can achieve! They are now probably struggling with the issues of Phase 4 growth, but the entire management team would be the first to say that the only certainty in their organization is that whatever is right for them now will be wrong in the future. They are already anticipating the next challenge of growth and the next set of rapids, or crisis, which will spell both threat and opportunity to the business. For example, as Innovex moves from being a national to an international business it is struggling with the issues of how to establish an international culture which transcends national boundaries, how to develop and empower managers who are already 100 per cent stretched, how to put reward, career development and recruitment systems in place which are appropriate to their international marketplace.

1.3.2   Phase 2: growth through direction

At this stage a strong leader is needed to provide a sense of focus and put in the basic budgeting, reward, communications systems needed for efficiency. Often the founder is temperamentally un-suited to this job and must pass it to a professional manager. But the very success of Phase 2 growth creates the seeds which make a second revolution inevitable. The directive 'top-down' management style starts to clash with the desire of professional managers to get on with managing their particular sphere of operations, where they are after all the 'expert'. Typically, such managers will get involved in a power-struggle to make their voice heard, or will become demotivated and leave. The crisis of autonomy has arrived.

Agrafax: preventing cardiac arrest

Agrafax, a successful agricultural PR agency established in Shrop-shire for fourteen years, has thirty-eight employees and a turnover of £1.5 million. Chairman and founder Mike Evans explains how the crisis of autonomy arrived:

> The people within are a high calibre, talented bunch but there are signs of stress, of blood pressure rising. Recruitment difficulties [in Shropshire] are restricting the flow of new blood into the organization and the young blood, who are all very highly motivated, are putting pressure on for more autonomy, less restriction from above, more say in strategy, more initiative and greater reward.

Mike Evans resolved the crisis of autonomy by giving space to his most valuable resource: people. He created account managers and account directors from among his up and coming Young Turks, he moved away from a hierarchical functional organization towards a more flexible matrix-type network, he started to look at the possibilities of share-ownership. Of course, in time, his solutions created new problems – some of the original team with whom Mike had established the business felt displaced and increasingly it became difficult to give the business a sharp strategic focus when so many young managers were 'doing their own thing'. But again, Mike shares the Greiner framework with his team and they all recognize that as the business continues its successful growth, the right answers don't stay right for very long.

1.3.3 Phase 3: growth through delegation

The solution to the crisis of autonomy lies in recognizing that more responsibility has to be delegated to more people in the company. The company needs a team, it needs to empower more people to get on with the decisions previously reserved for their owner/founder. As Agrafax found out, delegating decisions to give people a strong sense of involvement inevitably leads to control problems as the centre of the organization panics and tries to pull back power. Many organizations are struggling with the empowerment trap.

The Cranfield Business Growth Programme helps owner/founders and managers grow their businesses through Greiner's Phases 1–5. The programme is aimed at small businesses with under £10 million turnover. Very typically such businesses put themselves at Phase 3 development, identifying issues to do with team-building and delegation. Many such entrepreneurs identify dilemmas associated with their reluctance to let go of information, of power, of familiarity, of status.

Nor is the empowerment trap reserved for small businesses. Many blue-chip organizations are struggling with the dilemmas of pushing responsibility down. Managers all over the place are opening the windows and telling their staff to 'fly'. The casualties merely reinforce their belief that empowerment doesn't work anyway! In fact, as we start to understand what empowerment really means, it becomes clear that there are many issues to manage, for example:

- What are the 'givens', the boundaries which define the decisions people can't make for themselves?
- How willing are managers to let go of power?
- How much confidence do those who are 'empowered' have that they will be trained, supported, encouraged and rewarded?

- When times get hard do top managers panic and pull back the power?

1.3.4   Phase 4: growth through co-ordination

During the fourth growth phase the crisis of control can be overcome by achieving the best of both the delegative and the directive phases. Strategic planning processes attempt to combine both 'bottom-up' and 'top-down' planning methods. Systems and policies are developed to regulate the behaviour of managers at all levels. Communication is vital and a corporate culture takes shape giving employees a new feel for the way things are done in the company. This growth phase usually ends in a crisis of red tape where bureaucracy and clutter take over to stifle innovation and local initiative.

BP Oil: culture-change programme

BP's high-visibility culture-change programme of the early 1990s is a marvellous example of tuning in to the need for change and trying to orchestrate a co-ordinated response across some 120,000 people. BP Oil alone consists of some 58,000 people worldwide. When Chris Lorenz wrote up the BP story in the *Financial Times* this is how his notes described the need for change:

> November 8th meeting takes Horton through team's detailed analysis in diagrammatic form of the 'Why Change?'. Itemizes external threats and internal inadequacies on many fronts including the risk of becoming 'the dinosaur of the 90's'. Stresses need for BP to become more of a 'learning organization'. Also paints a vivid picture of dramatic gulf between the necessary future organization and the current reality. The deal embodies clear vision, continuous innovation, open communication, empowered people, deep trust, team accountability. The reality is lack of shared vision, confused messages, excessive emphasis on asset trading, breakdown in trust, lack of pride in BP.

BP encouraged its managers and teams across the world to identify for themselves the pressures for change in five key environmental areas:

1. Customers/markets.
2. Competitors.

3. Suppliers.
4. Community.
5. Employees.

Its 'values wheel' made positive statements about how the corporation intended to cope with each group of 'stakeholder'.

BP Oil went on to run literally hundreds of 'leading change workshops' all over the world in an attempt to co-ordinate an orchestrated international response to change. The crisis of red tape was never far away as the corporation struggled with the paradox of how to impose change top-down while encouraging bottom-up change initiatives from country managers in environments as different as Turkey, Germany, Spain, the United Kingdom, Scandinavia and Greece. In some cases, rather than international issues, the reality for local managers was how to get the new sets of overalls their petrol pump attendants had been promised. This focus on customers and pound notes didn't always mesh with the message from a still highly bureaucratic centre.

In many cases the greatest successes, such as BP Benelux, were where work groups had been set free to define their own environment, organization improvements, local values and programmes for change – true empowerment and bottom-up change.

In conclusion, it is interesting to note that Shell was recently reported as having rejected the argument for 'empowerment' as irrelevant to a huge multinational dealing in a commodity where they believe the rules can be defined at the centre. It will be interesting to see which view prevails!

1.3.5 Phase 5: growth through collaboration

The way to circumvent red tape as the organization grows bigger and older is to inculcate an attitude of collaboration throughout the organization. This calls for simplifying and integrating information flows horizontally *across* the organization and an emphasis on team-oriented activities, often of temporary multidisciplinary projects teams. This phase of growth contains many of the issues with which sophisticated businessmen will be wrestling through the 1990s, for example:

- How to manage and reward project team activity.
- How to manage the plethora of new information technology for effective communications.

- How to create networks across the organization.
- How to give people 'horizontal' opportunities for growth and progression.

1.4   Businesses with a buzz

What the business was yesterday isn't what it is today or will be tomorrow. The Chinese have two words for 'crisis'. These translate literally as 'dangerous opportunity'. But there's good news too. 'Crisis' means potential for growth as well as threat. It means buzz, excitement and challenge. Every 'threat' from the business environment can also provide the opportunity for positive change.

Anita Roddick: The Body Shop buzz

Body Shop has been *the* phenomenal success story of the 1980s, growing from a £4,000 investment in 1976 to an £8 million flotation by 1984. Anita Roddick foresaw the move towards environmentally friendly products and capitalized on it. She says: 'I get a real buzz from doing things differently from everyone else. We will be a vehicle for challenge and change.'

1.5   Scanning your business environment

The signals for change are always there: what's difficult for most businesses is to find ways of reading them. This means monitoring the business environment continuously and ensuring that feedback is listened to, even when the messages are unwelcome. It is not just shareholders who need to be tuned in to, but all the other stakeholders in the business. The analogy of a radar scan is a useful one. In scanning the radar screen one identifies 'blips' in time to do something about them. If the 'blips' turn out to be super-tankers then at least there is a better chance of taking evasive action. If the 'blip' is only a seagull, then time will tell and no harm done.

Sophie Mirman and Sock Shop

Of course we made mistakes, the biggest was our expansion into America. But we had an awful lot of bad luck at home. Two hot summers, which depressed hosiery sales, combined with a series of train and tube strikes, which kept so many of our shops closed one day each week over several months. And on top of that interest rates doubled to 15 per cent. Any one of these factors we could have coped with but not all of them together. And there was absolutely nothing we could do about any of them. I felt like a rabbit caught in headlights. (Sophie Mirman)

We might ask whether there is any such thing as 'bad luck' in business. Certainly, managers can increase the odds in favour of good luck by developing mechanisms which plug them into their business environments and by the old-fashioned means of keeping eyes and ears open for the often ambiguous signals that something is changing.

EXERCISE 1

SCANNING YOUR BUSINESS ENVIRONMENT

Q1 Identify the major business challenges and opportunities facing your organization. (You will naturally focus on the market and shareholder environment but don't forget other key groups such as employees and suppliers.) What are the implications for strategy, people, systems or structure?

Q2 What mechanisms does your business have in place to ensure continuous feedback from key customer groups?

Q3 How does your organization monitor and assess the significance of social, economic, political and technological developments?

Q4 Where would you place your business on the Greiner growth model? Please complete the organization development diagnostic questionnaire.

ORGANIZATIONAL DEVELOPMENT DIAGNOSTIC QUESTIONNAIRE

Instructions for completion

1. The organization development diagnostic consists of sixty descriptive statements. Your task is to work through this list and to identify those statements you believe to be accurate in describing your company.

2. Each time you come to an apt description you should tick it on the questionnaire. When you have looked through all sixty statements, please transfer the ticks to the score sheet, recording your choice on the score sheet by putting a tick in the box carrying the same number.
3. Add up your ticks and total them at the bottom. Around which vertical columns do your scores group? This would appear to be your diagnosis of your company's present stage of development. What are the inherent challenges you face?

1. The organizational structure is very informal. ☐
2. Top management are finding themselves bombarded with many unwanted management responsibilities. ☐
3. Management focus mainly on the efficiency of operations. ☐
4. Staff lower down in the organization possess more knowledge about, for example, markets, products, trends, etc., than do top management. ☐
5. The main management focus is to expand markets. ☐
6. Top management feel they are losing control of the business. ☐
7. The main management focus is co-ordination and consolidation. ☐
8. There is a lack of confidence between line managers and specialist staff/head office and the field. ☐
9. The main focus of management is on problem-solving and innovation. ☐
10. There is an overemphasis on teamwork. ☐
11. The top management style is very individualistic and entrepreneurial. ☐
12. Top management takes too long in responding to queries and requests. ☐
13. The organizational structure is centralized and functional, i.e. based on specialism. ☐
14. There is not enough freedom to act delegated to those capable of doing so. ☐
15. The organization structure is decentralized and individual divisions or departments have a high level of autonomy. ☐
16. Many people at lower levels have too much freedom to run their own show. ☐
17. Decentralized units have been merged into product groups. ☐
18. Line managers resent heavy staff direction. ☐
19. The organization is a matrix of task or project teams. ☐
20. There is dependency on group-think to the extent that some managers are losing the confidence to make individual decisions. ☐
21. The main control system is whether or not the sales targets are met. ☐

22. Top management do not provide enough direction. ☐
23. Top management style tends to be directive. ☐
24. Management tends to be over-directive and could easily delegate. ☐
25. The top management style is delegative. ☐
26. The organization has probably become too decentralized, breeding parochial attitudes. ☐
27. The top management style is to be a watchdog. ☐
28. We seem to have lost the ability to respond to new situations or solve problems quickly. ☐
29. The top management style is highly consultative, meeting together frequently on problem issues. ☐
30. We are directing too much energy into the functions of our internal teams and tending to overlook what is happening in the outside world. ☐
31. Long hours are rewarded by modest salaries but with the promise of ownership benefits in the future. ☐
32. Top management aren't as visible as they ought to be. ☐
33. The main control systems seem to be concerned with standards and costs. ☐
34. Flexibility suffers because those who could take decisions have to wait for management to agree. ☐
35. The main control seems to be in the form of profit-centre reporting. ☐
36. Power seems to have shifted away from top management. ☐
37. Each product group is an investment centre with extensive planning controls. ☐
38. Everyone is criticizing the bureaucratic paper system that has evolved. ☐
39. The main control system is for work groups to evaluate their own performance through real-time information systems integrated into daily work. ☐
40. There is almost too much personal feedback about behaviour at meetings, etc. ☐
41. The management focus is mainly on making and selling. ☐
42. Top management are very harassed; conflicts between them are growing. ☐
43. The main way managers are rewarded is by salary and merit increases. ☐
44. People are demotivated, even leaving, because they do not have enough personal autonomy in their jobs. ☐
45. The way managers are rewarded is by individual bonuses. ☐
46. More co-ordination of operations is needed if things are to improve. ☐
47. The way managers are rewarded is through profit-sharing and stock options. ☐
48. Fun and excitement seem to be lacking in the company. ☐

49. Rewards are geared more to team performance than to individual achievement. □

50. The constant high expectation for creativity in the organization is stressful. □

51. Top management are close to customers and have a good understanding of what the market requires. □

52. Top managers do not seem able to introduce the new business techniques which are necessary. □

53. To get on in this company, lower managers do not question decisions made by their seniors. □

54. Staff have their performance appraisals from bosses who have little understanding about the subordinate's job and work problems. □

55. People are told what is expected of them and then allowed to get on with their jobs as they see fit. It's management by exception. □

56. Senior managers are continually checking up to make sure that jobs are completed – they tend to overdo this. □

57. There are many head office personnel who initiate company work programmes to review and control line managers. □

58. Too many people are working to the book. □

59. Interpersonal conflicts are brought into the open and, on the whole, managed in a non-destructive way. □

60. Trying always to be spontaneous and open in relationships at work is proving stressful. □

Source: Adapted from John Leppard (1987).

Organization Development Diagnostic Score Sheet

Phase 1 Growth through creativity	1 Crisis of leadership	Phase 2 Growth through direction	2 Crisis of autonomy	Phase 3 Growth through delegation	3 Crisis of control	Phase 4 Growth through co-ordination	4 Crisis of red tape	Phase 5 Growth through collaboration	5 Crisis of ?
1	2	3	4	5	6	7	8	9	10
11	12	13	14	15	16	17	18	19	20
21	22	23	24	25	26	27	28	29	30
31	32	33	34	35	36	37	38	39	40
41	42	43	44	45	46	47	48	49	50
51	52	53	54	55	56	57	58	59	60

1.6 Summary

Change is the very essence of business growth – it's inevitable and unavoidable. Stability is an illusion. The rate of change has accelerated over the last decade, external environmental pressures are driving change at an alarming rate and affecting every aspect of our lives, politically, socially, organizationally. Identifying environmental and market changes quickly and opportunistically is part of the key to survival and growth. But managing change has now also become a crucial element of competitive advantage, for it is only by guiding people through change as fast and as painlessly as possible that the organization can hope to respond to market pressures before the world moves on. The start point for managing change comes from helping everyone to understand why change is necessary in the first place. Historical success no longer guarantees future survival and the past can no longer predict the future. 'More of the same' doesn't work anymore, we must map new futures and reinvent ourselves. Businesses go through predictable stages of evolution and revolution, and need to change at each stage, or go under. Change is continuous, there is no arrival point. But at least we can anticipate and plan for the challenges of each phase of development. Change represents opportunity as well as threat, it can be fun. As the only alternative is to be boiled alive, we might as well get on with it. The start point for change managers is to work with their team in identifying the demands of the environment on the business.

2

Diagnose organization capability

Having tuned in to the external drivers for change, the second key element of the change process, vital to producing sustainable change, is to diagnose your organization's capability to deliver the kinds of changes which the marketplace and external world demand. To sustain change we need to develop an understanding of what makes organizations tick. However clear the message of change, the organization is the only medium through which performance can be delivered. Too few leaders really understand this. Saying it doesn't make it happen. Much of the frustration of chief executives lies here. They know what needs to be changed but they cannot get the organization to move fast enough. However, once we understand the power of organizations, the sources of inertia can become levers for change.

Quick fixes, or changes based on a one-dimensional recipe – typically restructuring – rarely work. To avoid changes which are merely cosmetic or nine-day wonders, managers have to change the organization extensively and deeply across all aspects of structure, systems, people, style and culture.

In this chapter we will introduce a model of organization which will help you understand and analyze your organizational resource, building up a picture of where you are, where you're going and what agenda for change will get you there. You will be able to pinpoint which aspects of your organization fit your plans for change and which aspects will themselves need to be changed to reinforce what you are trying to do.

Managers also need to be able to direct the use of an appropriate range of 'levers' to bring about change. Pulling the 'structure' lever may look easy but does not always produce sustainable change. Those who create change by trying to change the formal structure alone can get nasty shocks because they have unwittingly disrupted informal networks and politics.

2.1   The challenge of the 1990s

Shaping up to the challenge of the 1990s poses a key dilemma. How do we create organizations which can respond simultaneously on at least two dimensions – first, in meeting the specific needs of local markets; second, in orchestrating a corporate response to a market-place which is increasingly international, or global?

It is an interesting dilemma. The pressures of mass production and the drive to standardization work in the direction of a transnational product: like the car, or the video recorder or a bottle of 'cola'. At the same time, customers are much more choosy and have higher expectations about the product 'tailoring', the add-ons which suit their personal preferences, pocket and local customs, and they expect choice and variety at a mass-production price. So it is the mix of low cost versus high variety products which provides the challenge.

It is likely that there will always be a tension between these two requirements. Local responsiveness argues for small business units and autonomous management who can tune in to a specific group of customers and respond fast to their changing needs. Local responsiveness suggests a Phase 1-type 'entrepreneurial' business start-up – young, vibrant, closely in touch. By contrast, maintaining global presence requires a weightier, mature organization, which can provide a consistent response and behave with integrity across all its businesses – probably more like a Phase 3–Phase 5 organization.

Effective organization used to be about size and economies of scale. Being the biggest and the cheapest provided insurmountable barriers to entry. In a mass-production company, jobs were interchangeable, an employee no more than a unit of production. That's no longer true. The scarce resource in tomorrow's organization is 'know-how', the major challenge that of transporting the unique raw material of people across the boundaries of products, countries, markets and functions. This is demanding a new kind of organization to maximize core competencies as well as core businesses, often where the manager nurturing and developing the skills is developing them for others to use, as in a matrix-type consulting engineering business. Managers have to exert influence without line authority, often on only a temporary basis and frequently across great distances of geography, language and customs.

BICC Technology Group: establishing global reach

In the late 1980s Mike Watson, then managing director of BICC Technologies, a group of electronics and communications companies with a turnover of £200 million and sitting within the huge multinational BICC cables group, was searching for a way of addressing the problem of global niche markets and establishing 'global reach'.

Each of his five technology businesses were players in several countries – the United Kingdom, France, Germany and the United States among them. The traditional approach had been for each business, expensively and often with little local presence, to set up its own, for example, French subsidiary.

The option he preferred was to develop a lower cost, more flexible federated approach with one only of the five businesses charged with establishing a BICC Technology 'umbrella' company in a specific country as a way of providing a 'starter kit' for the development of new business – a starter kit containing legal identity, PR and marketing presence, local office facilities, accounting services and even shared exhibitions.

BICC offers some clues on the shape of the future and also touches on some of the organizational levers for change in the new world. More and more, people are becoming a key lever for change, particularly if we can learn how to make them a much more flexible resource which can be rapidly allocated to new projects, new products and new countries, probably on a temporary basis. This may mean forgetting the old, upward hierarchy and promotion prospects and adopting career progression based on acquiring a portfolio of skills.

The challenge to substantial organizations is therefore how to create autonomous businesses which behave entrepreneurially within a shared international framework of values, standards and procedures. It is interesting that in the early 1980s ICL ran into exactly this type of dilemma when it reorganized a functional hierarchy into independent businesses aligned with specific market segments, for example: retail, government and health care. There were often fierce power-struggles between the business unit managers attempting to behave like feudal barons and the centre trying to retain control – the pressure to centralize, the pressure to delegate and 'let go' versus the necessity to define the 'givens' within which people operate.

2.2 Organizing for change

The model of organization illustrated in Figure 2.1 helps us to understand just how much is involved in creating sustainable change. Understanding what is happening in the business environment is only the start point. Many people think of 'strategy' purely as the definition of the key external challenges to which the business chooses to respond. But the arrows point both ways:

ENVIRONMENT ↔ STRATEGY ↔ ORGANIZATION

Without the organizational capability to make it happen there can be no deliverable strategy for change. So putting in place an effective strategy for change means:

1. Assessing our existing organizational capability in terms of current people skills/style, systems and structure.
2. Deciding whether what we've currently got fits the direction in which we're trying to move the business.
3. Identifying the 'misfits' and translating them into our internal agenda for change.
4. Deciding which levers to pull to make change happen: Strategy? Structure? People? Or Systems?

If one regards 'strategy' as the matching of organization resource (people, systems and structure) to environmental opportunity, then it becomes clear that every time there is an environmental/strategic shift in emphasis, then the different parts of the organization will also need to change gear. The 'people', 'systems' and 'structure' elements are like plates spinning on sticks – there is always a danger that one plate is wobbling terminally and needs an urgent tweak to keep it in place. All these parts of the organization interlink so that a change in, for example, structure will have implications for the systems used and also for management style. The question of 'fit' is vital:

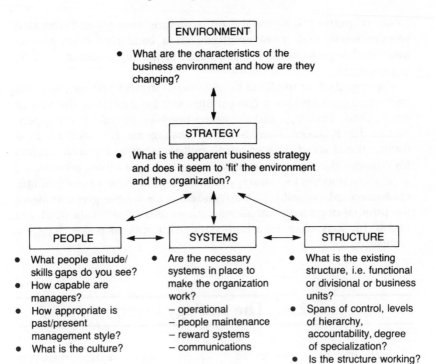

Figure 2.1 Organizing for change

- When IBM, having made the largest loss in corporate history, tried desperately to reshape itself for a new world, its very size and the strength of its culture worked against the quest for flexibility.

- When Robb Wilmot, managing director of ICL, in 1981 tried to move an organization of 20,000 people towards his strategy for survival, he found an immensely frustrating misfit of resistance from his management team who hoped change would go away.

- When George Davies was removed from the Board of Directors of Next there was a well-publicized personality clash and management style misfit.

- When Sear Holdings tried to diversify into new markets it encountered a major structure misfit as its highly centralized 'super-tanker' shape failed to allow a fast response to customers.

Any of these elements of the organization can provide the appropriate lever for change. In general, the organization of the

1990s is putting less weight on structure change and constant reorganization and more emphasis on a combination of people/ process change to achieve realignment of the organization with its environment.

The organization model of environment, strategy, people, systems and structure provides a good framework for assessing the size of your change challenge and the issues involved in making it happen. Figure 2.2 is taken from a senior management workshop in a multinational which was trying to pull together a corporate agenda for change. The numbers indicate their top six priorities, three in the area of environment ↔ strategy fit and three in the area of providing organizational capability. One wonders if they have given some of the internal organizational issues such as relocation, skills shortages and technology changes a high enough priority to make change a reality.

2.3   The strategy lever

Though the corporate guiding 'vision' should remain relatively constant, it is likely that constant realignment of business strategy will be needed as marketplaces shift. Every era has its fads – in the 1960s it was merger and acquisition, in the 1970s diversification, in the 1980s the pendulum swung back to merger and acquisitions. Through the 1990s some distinct refocusing on core businesses is likely as companies hit by the recession decide to go back to basics, as did Prudential Assurance in getting out of a disastrous flirtation with estate agencies, and Ericsson (Sweden) in dumping its mis-alliance with a computer business. 'Stick to the knitting' seems to be the rallying cry, with a distinct emphasis on exploring as a first line of attack the possibilities of the current marketplace and current products rather than the risky business of diversification.

Formulating strategy is becoming a much more pragmatic affair than it was in the heady days of ivory tower corporate planning departments. As one cynic says: 'Whatever you hit you call your strategy.' The responsibility for corporate strategy still rests at the top with the chief executive, but despite helicopter vision, the world is now far too complex for one person to predict. Therefore, the responsibility for strategic change is becoming more and more diffused through the organization, 'bottom-up' as well as 'top-down'.

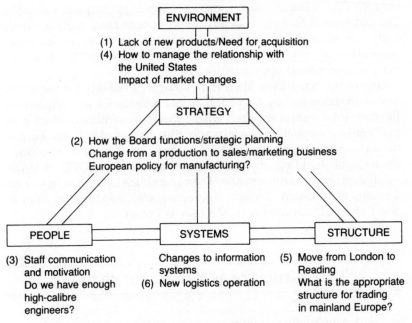

ENVIRONMENT

(1) Lack of new products/Need for acquisition
(4) How to manage the relationship with
    the United States
    Impact of market changes

STRATEGY

(2) How the Board functions/strategic planning
    Change from a production to sales/marketing business
    European policy for manufacturing?

PEOPLE

(3) Staff communication
    and motivation
    Do we have enough
    high-calibre
    engineers?

SYSTEMS

Changes to information
    systems
(6) New logistics operation

STRUCTURE

(5) Move from London to
    Reading
    What is the appropriate
    structure for trading
    in mainland Europe?

Figure 2.2 Identifying a corporate agenda for change

This is creating an interesting organization dilemma as there is still a widely-held expectation among staff and middle management that someone else will define the strategy and tell them what to do. Often, therefore, there is an impassioned cry for top management to provide more clarity of strategic direction just at the point where the pace of change and its inherent ambiguity is making this almost impossible. It is as though every Board of Directors is supposed to have a template for change in a secret desk drawer spelling out in reassuring detail exactly where the business is going over the next five years. That's no longer possible. An eminent professor, talking about the future of one of the major UK institutions, says:

> There is no blueprint guiding where it is going. No one knows what it will look like in 3 to 4 years, we're making it up as we go along. There is still uncertainty about what will emerge, so if you're confused, that's OK. It's all to play for as the changes go forward.

What is needed is a mind-shift which encourages every manager to be a leader in his or her own right, managing part of the organization resources and capable of input to strategic thinking. The old type of strategy is dead. Tactical pragmatism wins the day, with a high emphasis on the tactics of cash management and cash generation as a way of allowing organizations the flexibility to exploit their market opportunities fast.

One of the remarkable themes of strategic flexibility for the 1990s lies in massive link-ups across national boundaries and expansion through joint ventures, often where the joint venture partner was previously a competitor, for example, the merger of ICL and Fujitsu in the mid-1980s to the mid-1990s and Sir Arnold Weinstock's strategy of building the different businesses of GEC through significant joint ventures: the Telecommunications business with Siemens in Germany, Power Engineering with Alsthrom in France, and Defence Electronics with MATRA in France.

2.4   Structure as a lever for change

To most people, organization structure means organization chart: a pattern of boxes and lines reflecting a traditional functional, hierarchical organization with the boss at the top, small spans of control, lots of levels of hierarchy, clearly defined jobs and a poor old 'me' at the bottom of the pile. The mythology associated with this kind of thinking is based on the misleading assumption that the organization chart has an absolute reality. It leads us into the temptation of believing that changing organization means changing structure and that changing structure is as easy as pinning up a new organization chart with new boxes and dotted lines.

Structure is much more than an organization chart. Organization charts indicate the formal reporting relationships, but they don't show how things actually work, who is influential, where the power lies, how the politics can be used to make change happen. They don't show the physical structure: in which buildings people work, the size of their office, how near they are to the nexus of power or the reality of the internal relationships which spring up around the coffee machine. And yet it is these things which actually determine the reality of how people relate to each other and therefore how momentum for change can be created.

Effective change will mean harnessing the informal as well as the formal structure. Tandem Computers have understood this point well in creating 'beer busts', weekly informal gatherings everywhere in the world at 3 p.m. on a Friday, a chance to unwind but also a chance to lobby, relate, leverage, connect.

Reorganizations can be a powerful lever for change in putting the resource where you need it; for example, restructuring into 'business centres' which are closely aligned with particular customer groups. Reorganizations also give strong signals to both customers and employees that things are changing. Thus when Innovex, of whom we spoke earlier, reorganized in the early 1990s from thirteen functions into five focused customer areas they improved both their customer responsiveness and their internal efficiency.

But sometimes structure change becomes too obvious a choice, without other levers being considered; it can then become a case of rearranging the deck-chairs on the *Titanic* – disruptive and also ultimately unproductive.

If structure change is to be used effectively, it must be used within the context of informal as well as formal structures and within the changing shape of organizations in the 1990s.

Some of the flavour of the new structures is seen in the move towards:

- Flat organization.
- Customer-centred organization.
- Network organization.
- Cellular organization.

2.4.1 Flat organization

The old organization structures have been turned on their heads, sweeping away layers of management, cutting back sprawling HQs. Vertical, functional structures no longer work. They were great for stable environments but are hopeless for situations of dynamic change. With them goes the traditional organization chart. It is interesting that many businesses have either scrapped their old organograms or started to depict their structure in a new way. They are asking the question: 'Where is the customer on the organization chart?' Instead of an organization consisting of a number of departmental empires, set up for the good of those within them, many organizations are regarding the organization's only rationale as support to the front line so that all resources are allocated with the customer in mind. The Ind Coope Burton Brewery has redesigned its structure as a series of interlocking teams with no clear hierarchy. Appropriately, their structure is said to reflect fermenting beer as seen through a microscope!

A recent memo from the new American CEO of a huge multinational to its outposts in Europe said: 'There will be no hierarchy: the executive committee is disbanded.' While this may be somewhat of an exaggeration, there is a crystal-clear trend in all major organizations in the 1990s to reduce levels of management, hopefully cutting out unnecessary cost and improving communication flow up and down and more particularly across the organization. In its three UK manufacturing sites, for example, Glaxo Pharmaceuticals has cut back a factory hierarchy of eight levels to four, doing away with the 'deputy to', 'assistant to', 'foreman', 'chargehand'-type nomenclature to simple operational units with team leaders. Skyscraper organization hierarchies are becoming, instead, a series of interconnected bungalows.

2.4.2   Customer-centred organization

Another clear trend in the shape of the future is to move from structures with the traditional functional dimensions – for example, marketing/manufacturing/sales – towards structures which get you closer to the customer, and are therefore divided up to reflect different markets rather than different functions. It is interesting to see how seriously organizations are taking the customer. The managing director of Habitat (now part of the Swedish Group IKEA), talking about the company's revamped strategy to recapture its traditional middle-class market, has insisted that every manager spends at least two days with customers in the field – the place where understanding the business starts.

2.4.3   Network organization

Traditionally, the important flows of information have been up and down the hierarchy. However, the recent focus on total quality and customer responsiveness puts great emphasis on horizontal processes which, through various elements of the customer/supplier chain, lead eventually to the end-user. Everyone is someone else's customer. People are having to learn to work together across functional boundaries after years of calling each other the enemy. One of the challenges of the 1990s is to overcome the rigid stratification of the old-style organization in increasing fluidity, breaking down internal barriers and disseminating knowledge. Information technology is a great enabler, allowing Digital, for example, to put together a team from all over the world, dialling into one database.

'Networking' frequently manifests itself in the creation of temporary project teams – drawing people in from a multidisciplinary background. Few organizations yet know how to manage project teams like these. Frequently, their creativity, authority and power are stifled by 'plugging' them too rigidly into a formal reporting process to top management, ensuring that the most senior person chairs the project team and pulling the teeth of their recommendations.

Charles Hardy, author of *The Age of Unreason*, is an influential thinker on organizations of the future. He describes the 'network' organization, rather graphically, as consisting of a series of teams or 'eggs', which must form their own connections with other 'eggs'. Innovation necessitates building synergy across the organization – the $1 + 1 = 3$ effect.

2.4.4   Cellular organization

The new organization consists of a collection of small teams, each with a high degree of autonomy, like the Dutch BSO, a highly successful software house of getting on for 2,000 people. Every time a group gets up to around fifty people in size, it 'buds' off to form a cell on its own. In BSO each 'cell' is totally responsible for all aspects of the business except payroll; there are no central staff departments.

'Power/distance' the difference in social standing of leader and follower is getting less. Each member of the team has a high sense of ownership and responsibility for the team's output. Self-policing replaces imposed supervision. For example, it is interesting how many organizations are now using the work of Dr Meredith Belbin on the eight roles of effective teams, encouraging individuals not just to label themselves with one role in a team, for example 'Shaper' (leader) or 'Plant' (creative thinker), but to develop the maturity to move into different roles as required for a successful team mix.

2.5   Systems can be sexy

Many of the changes organizations experience in the 1990s will be both precipitated by the impact of new developments in world technology and enabled by information technology and internal shifts in systems and processes. Unfortunately, business processes usually reflect what one needed historically rather than future or even current realities. The infrastructure is difficult to change and needs considerable attention from those at the top of the organization, who are probably the only ones with the power to make such changes.

Old systems can frequently be a drag on the ability of the organization to move forward with change – they just don't 'fit' any more. In the case of ICL, which we will examine in a later chapter, the dramatic strategic change away from mainframes to desktop systems in the mid-1980s, was seriously hampered by the old operational systems, perfectly suitable for tracking sales of a few mainframes but inappropriate to keeping tabs on the sales of many, much less expensive products to different user groups.

So the old systems can get in the way and impede change. In his attempts to change the culture of BP, Sir Robert Horton recognized lack of 'fit' of some key systems and commented:

- 'Desired changes in culture and behaviour won't come about until rewards reinforce the new BP values instead of the old.'
- 'Out current appraisal system is wholly deficient to tackle team working.'

However, because of their interconnections with other parts of the organization the good news is that systems can also drive change, like a small cog which can ratchet up other parts of the machine. Systems change, unlike structure changes, can also be a more gradual evolutionary change which doesn't raise resistance levels sky high and totally disrupt teams and relationships. As structure becomes less formal and more a matter of informal and temporary networks, one moves, inevitably, into systems rather than hierarchy as a co-ordinating mechanism.

Some particular aspects of systems which are likely to be on the agenda for change of businesses in the 1990s include:

- Reward systems.
- Career development systems.
- Appraisal systems.
- Communication systems.
- Operational systems.

2.5.1 Reward systems

It is said that what gets measured gets produced. And what gets rewarded gets produced again. The rule is: expect it and reward it or forget it! Sometimes we end up rewarding the old behaviours rather than those we are trying to encourage under the new regime.

Some of the levers to pull are likely to include:

- More emphasis on team as well as individual performance.
- Output orientation is all very well, but how can we reward people for a good try that doesn't come off? Without rewarding risk-taking there will be little innovation.
- More emphasis on rewarding the achievement of 'soft' people objectives as well as the more familiar 'hard' sales/profit/cost objectives.
- Designing reward systems to reinforce the value of cross-functional moves and secondments.
- Establishing 'cafeteria' benefit systems so that individuals can pick their own package.

2.5.2 Career development systems

The days when a young graduate, entering one of the great oil companies, would have his career path mapped out thirty years forward are well and truly gone. The old systems of developing neat succession charts are totally irrelevant to the key issues of the 1990s, which include:

- How do organizations keep people motivated as the organization gets flatter and the opportunities for advancement fewer?
- How can the expectations of the 'Young Turks' coming into the organization be managed?
- How can horizontal opportunities for career development be created?
- How can emphasis be placed on the individual's personal responsibility for actively managing his or her own career?
- Who gets on in the organization, and are they the people we want as 'heroes' and role models?

The concept of a job for life is outdated. Perhaps the best that companies can do in the future is to offer people 2 to 3 years' experience which will be enjoyable, stimulating and will add to the 'marketability' of that individual. For example, McKinsey, the famous consulting firm, adopt exactly this approach. Few make it to 'partner' status, but all leave richer for the experience and infinitely more employable.

2.5.3   Appraisal systems

Rethinking the appraisal system can have a powerful impact on management style and behaviour. Many of our large and prestigious organizations – McKinsey, Glaxo and BP among them – have redesigned their appraisal systems away from 'top-down' towards a large element of self-appraisal, peer appraisal and – most dramatic of all – upward appraisal of the boss, a test of an open culture if ever there was one!

2.5.4   Communication systems

Marvellous breakthroughs in technology have and will continue to revolutionize communications. Already we have electronic mail, video-conferencing – not too far away are the possibilities of seeing the person with whom you are networking. Yet it is not at all unusual for an individual returning from holiday to find 250 'voice-mails' on the desk. We are deluged with information. Advances in technology have given us a Pandora's box, full of good things but also something we cannot yet handle and which is clogging the organization with irrelevant information.

Waves of change will impact on organizations in this area, but they are also waves of change which involve not only pure technology but educating people in their use. Suspect new phenomena are emerging, electronic mail can cause 'flaming', spontaneous outbursts of graffiti! People who sit at the next desk are bombarding each other with mail messages. Face-to-face and informal communications are still the most powerful way of influencing each other. Are we using them? Is there anyone out there?

2.5.5   Operational systems

Obsolete systems have a terrible habit of lingering on years after they ceased to be useful. People almost develop an affection for them. When Prudential Assurance company salesmen were weaned away from their old 'blue book' towards new computer technology, there was much resistance, pain and loss and all for a few familiar pieces of paper.

The risk is that as long as people hang on to the old systems they will not have the time or energy wholeheartedly to welcome the new. Time is a very limited commodity. If we want people to behave in new ways, then they must drop some of the old, time-consuming habits. Every aspect of operational systems – sales invoicing, order processing, budgeting, stock control – will be challenged and audited to assess 'fit' with the new organization.

2.6   The people lever and culture change

If 'structure' is the skeleton of organization and 'process' represents the nervous system or infrastructure of the organization, then 'people' are the blood and guts! Without understanding and mobilizing the energies of teams and individuals, no change, however brilliant, will be sustainable. Understanding people, both as a source of inertia and a source of leverage for change, means understanding what your organization has and needs in the way of skills-mix, whether management attitudes and styles are appropriate for the future you're trying to create. It means asking questions like:

- Will the business need more/fewer marketeers, financial analysts, engineers, general managers in the future?
- Where will we get them from?
- Have we got enough managers to run a changed business, and do they have the business management skills to do so?
- What is the traditional/current management style (i.e. autocratic/ *laissez-faire*), and is this going to help or hinder our attempts to lead change?
- What are the morale levels of 'the troops', and how will change impact on them?

Most of all it means realizing that, unfortunately, the people resource you need to achieve your strategy for change cannot be put in place overnight. Whatever you do – retraining, redundancy, reskilling, recruitment – will take time, and therefore needs to be built in early to the critical path for change.

The same applies to culture change. In the business of making change, 'corporate culture' is a two-edged sword. 'Culture' is the organizational equivalent of the fingerprint, the unique identification of every business in terms of its history, assumptions, values and behaviours. Without a good understanding of the traditions which underlie a particular business it is all too easy to propose changes which completely go against the grain and will therefore be rejected by the body of the organization. Look, for example, at the problems which Sir Jocelyn Stevens encountered in trying to change English Heritage. What he was trying to do was probably very necessary, but 'the bull in the china shop' approach runs the risk not just of putting people's backs up, but ultimately of failing.

On the other hand, a lot of organizations are quite consciously using culture change as a positive weapon for change.

Culture change is hot news in the 1990s; there is a requirement to change 'the way we do things around here' to reflect new business realities. 'It is the ideas of a business which are controlling, not some manager with authority,' says Robert Haas, chief executive of Levi Strauss. As the old 'command and control' hierarchies get stripped away, businesses are developing a new set of attitudes and behaviours, a 'genetic code' which will help people to know how to behave in unchartered waters.

A strong culture can be regarded as the internal branding, which stamps the same value on the people of the organization as the company promotes in its PR to the external marketplace. Building a culture which is appropriate to a dynamic and changing marketplace is one of the new challenges:

> Culture not product. Increasingly, companies are having to market their culture or brand image, not simply their products, in order to beat their competitors. BMW and Sony sell an image called 'quality'; Britain's Body Shop sell 'environmental friendliness'. But this will convince consumers only if the appropriate culture thrives throughout the company. Japanese managers have this driven home to them throughout their careers; western business schools still find the idea hard to teach. But teach it they must. (*The Economist*, 2 March 1991)

The Prudential is trying to align its external and internal branding. It has spent a great deal of productive time and money on revamping its external face, with the new image of 'Prudence' and the much copied advertising campaign around 'I want to be . . .'. It is now attempting to align the internal culture with the marketplace, although sometimes its long history works against change.

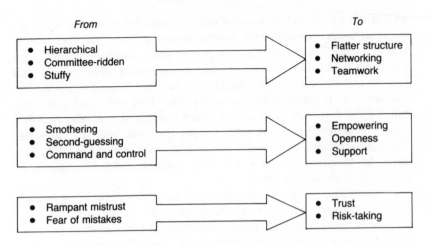

Figure 2.3 The changing BP culture

In companies that have a strong culture 'the way we do things around here' is clearly articulated, passionately communicated and understood by even the newest recruit. After all, 'culture' is what people do when and where there is nobody to check!

Organizations are being transformed out of all recognition. Part of this transformation lies in trying to realign internal behaviours with external requirements. Values can be the motor for change. Major programmes of 'culture change' took place in the 1980s within British Airways, ICL, SAS. The 1990s have seen the much publicized example of BP trying to get away from its imperial heritage and 'command and control' structure by creating a more flexible, flatter 'delayered' organization. As Figure 2.3 indicates, they are trying to re-engineer the 'soft' side away from a stuffy bureaucracy of rampant mistrust and constant second-guessing to the values of 'openness, care, teamwork, empowerment and trust'.

Most people would say that BP is transforming itself successfully and that the changes were absolutely essential for business survival. However, as a lever for change, 'culture' has the disadvantage that it takes a great deal of time. (Folklore suggests at least five years for a major attitude shift.) It also demands a tremendous amount of reinforcement if the change is to be sustained against the inevitable tendency to regress to old behaviours when the going gets tough or the initiator of culture change moves on.

This means not only reinforcement in terms of management education to 'evangelize' the masses nor just realigning processes and structure. It means a major commitment from the top management to 'walk the talk' and demonstrate that they live the values. When the 'old' behaviours which people see around them clash with the hype which is coming from top management, then people will believe the actions not the words. We 'say' we believe in openness, but we 'see' political behaviours. We 'say' take risks and innovate, but we 'see' punitive measures taken against those who fail! We 'say' we believe in developing people, but we 'see' that it is the bastards who get promoted! These dilemmas are exceedingly difficult to manage. Perhaps a 'health warning' should come with attempts to change culture!

Like BP, Levi Strauss has become a major advocate of culture change. Robert Haas talks about the impact of an uncertain economic climate on traditional marketplaces and therefore the need to create new, less passive behaviours, which make the 'supertanker' organization easier to turn as market opportunities emerge.

As we've outlined, there are many paradoxes inherent in these attempts to change culture and the jury is still out in terms of how successful such change initiatives will prove to be. Can a 'culture' which has been well established for many years be changed? How can people be told top-down that they will participate! Is it even worth trying to establish a 'new' corporate culture as a major change programme? Might a more local look at 'how we do business' be more appropriate? However, what is crystal clear is that whether it is perceived as a positive driver for change or the traditions which can stop change from gelling, managers who want to make changes must understand the culture they are working within.

2.7 Managing for the future

Much academic research, for example at Ashridge Management Centre and by Columbia University/Korn Ferry in the United States, indicates that the job of managing in the 1990s will be almost unrecognizable from traditional management. The role of management in organizations is being rewritten. The Ashridge Management research project suggests that 'managers will, in future, have to operate in organizational environments that are growth- and customer-oriented, faster moving, increasingly international and demand much greater responsibility, initiative and leadership from managers at all levels of the organization'.

The changing context of management will impact on how we look at the job of managing. Some of the likely trends will be towards:

- The manager as 'sensor' of the environment.
- From vertical to horizontal management.
- Leadership necessary at all levels in the organization.
- Manager as 'animateur'/catalyst.
- Changes in time-horizon from short to longer term.
- Rebalancing the importance of work and private life.
- Impact of information flow and use of it.

The Korn Ferry/Columbia University research indicates that the day when the salesman or saleswoman was pre-eminent, or the accountant's financial skills were the 'core' requirement of successful management, are gone. The effective leader will need, in order of importance, four key areas of expertise:

1. Strategy formulation.
2. Human resource management.
3. Marketing/sales.
4. Negotiation/conflict resolution.

The role of the leader is moving from soldier to strategist; his or her personal characteristics must change accordingly from the tough aggressive robber-barons of the early twentieth century to the creative, inspirational CEO of the twenty-first.

It is the small, day-to-day actions of managers which add up to become the 'macro'-level culture. Management style is a key issue, and changing management style can be a powerful way of getting change in an organization. This obviously and frequently occurs at the top of organizations when there is a misfit between the CEO's management style and the values of the rest of the management team. A notable example was the removal of Sir Robert Horton from BP.

2.8   Identifying your agenda for change

It can be very productive to bring together a team of managers to identify the key issues of change which concern the business.

Exercise 2 provides you with a blank 'pro forma', which you can use to 'diagnose' your organization. Determining a priority order for the changes, based on an allocation of points, can provide a useful focus on what needs to be addressed.

EXERCISE 2

IDENTIFYING YOUR AGENDA FOR CHANGE

1. What are the main characteristics of your organization at present?

Environment

Strategy

People   *Systems*   *Structure*

---   ---   ---

---   ---   ---

---   ---   ---

2. What are the major 'fits' (√) and 'misfits' (X) between these different parts of the organization?

3. Having examined the 'misfits' what 4–5 key items would you transfer to your organization agenda for change? Do these, for example, lie in the areas of reward systems, or strategy, or management style, or structure?

2.9 Summary

Chapter 1 examined the turbulence of the business environment which creates the reason why change is inevitable and unavoidable. But change can only happen through the organization. This chapter has provided some clues to understanding both the inertia and the leverage which the organization can provide. It also suggests what is likely to be on the agenda for change of the organization of the

1990s. One of the key challenges is how to design an organization which can tailor its products and services to be responsive to local customer needs, while maintaining a global culture and presence. Organization change doesn't just mean structure change, although we can expect some reorganization as businesses slim down, get closer to their customers and become networks of teams. We can also expect shifts in strategy formulation down the organization and towards the tactical pragmatism of joint ventures and retrenchment. Changing technology is both part of the demand system and also an enabler in realigning operational, people and information systems to meet new market requirements. Changing values or 'culture' is becoming a key driver for change and, on a more local level, the job of the manager of the 1990s is being transformed. 'Fit' of the different parts of the organization one with another and with the external reality is vital. It is impossible to change one part of the organization without knock-on effects. Managers will want to identify and plan for these changes and develop a robust and focused agenda for change.

3

Change starts with you

3.1 Adjust your mind-set

So far, in developing the elements of a change process, we've been operating at a global level in identifying the external drivers for change and diagnosing internal organizational capability. Yet you personally are one of the most powerful levers for change: your attitudes, your enthusiasm, your willingness to allow people's reactions to change the change as it goes along, the way you 'role model' the kinds of new behaviours you are seeking, your vulnerability and willingness to change yourself. How indeed can you change other people's mind-sets unless you are prepared to challenge your own?

This chapter will help you think about and challenge your own assumptions, assess your personal leadership style and give you some tools and techniques for helping others to 'grind new eyeglasses' and see the world differently.

Whether you are reorganizing, making an acquisition, relocating your business or introducing technology change, the 'X' factor in a successful change will be YOU and your attitude. As Mikhail Gorbachev once said, 'We are all products of our time. If change is to happen we all have to change ourselves.' The shape of tomorrow is changing and fast. There isn't a fault in reality so it can only be that our personal mind-set needs adjusting. Whether you perceive change as a threat or opportunity, whether it excites or depresses you, it's all in the mind. Given that change is the only reality in life, as in business, it is extraordinary that we spend so much time and invest so much energy in trying to maintain the status quo. Many would say that the only really important job of the leader and professional manager is to make change happen, and to do this you may want to challenge your assumptions about the world. If you would like to do a spot-check on your own mind-set please turn to the light-hearted questionnaire, 'Paradigm Lost', included as part of Exercise 3 (p. 64) and check your 'consumption' of comfortable illusions! The third part of the exercise – understanding your underlying values – will help you see what motivates you and therefore how you are likely to react to changes which threaten your core values.

The lens through which we perceive the world is made up of our own attitudes and assumptions, which act as a filter on reality. As Adam Smith said: 'When we are in the middle of a paradigm it is hard to imagine any other paradigm.' This would not be a problem for businesses if they stayed in a single paradigm indefinitely. But given the accelerating pace of change, the life-expectancy of any one framework is getting shorter and shorter. There is no objective reality; the rules and regulations which define how we do business keep shifting.

When a paradigm shifts, the obvious and predictable are not what occurs. The old ways of doing things no longer work, doing more and better what you did before won't do the trick. Rather, we have radically to re-examine and throw out some of our comfortable old assumptions. As Marcel Proust said: 'The real act of discovery lies not in finding new lands but in seeing with new eyes.' Take the Swiss watch industry, for example. When there was a paradigm shift from mechanical watches to electronic technology the Japanese quickly recognized it, acted on the shift and captured the market. The Swiss didn't say 'the paradigm has shifted', instead they clung to the old rules and tried to create even better bearings and mainsprings: fiddling while Rome burnt. Their resistance isn't surprising. When you have been successful by the rules of the old game, there is no guarantee that you will be successful in the new, and this can create substantial anxiety. If we fail to achieve a mind-shift in our thinking, we will become the dinosaurs with the old worldview who cannot take advantage of a new order.

Accelerating rates of change pose us with a tremendous challenge of almost constantly reassessing and revaluing our personal assumptions and of developing considerable flexibility of thought: if there are two courses of action always take the third. We need to break out of the 'box', developing second-order problem-solving skills because we cannot solve problems at the same level of thought with

Join these nine dots with four straight lines without taking your pencil off the paper

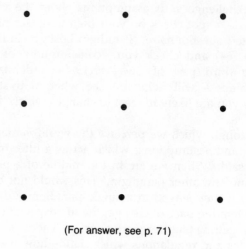

(For answer, see p. 71)

Figure 3.1 The nine dots problem

which we created them. A well-known example is the nine dots problem, shown in Figure 3.1, where the solution lies not in first-order thinking but in a radical shift of perspective outside the box formed by the pattern of dots.

When there is a paradigm shift, it's almost as if we have to transport ourselves to another planet from which we see both familiar and unfamiliar objects in a new light. When we choose to see the world in new ways we literally change the world that is there for us to see.

This is the essence of innovation. Take Tom Sawyer reframing the problem of being told that he can't go out to play but must repaint the picket fence in his garden. He shifted his paradigm from 'I'm miserable, I can't go out' to 'This is fun'. Suddenly it was fun! All his friends joined in and Tom as a budding entrepreneur had created the opportunity to charge them each sixpence for the pleasure!

Look at Midland First Direct Banking, a business which turned the rules on their head, creating sustainable competitive advantage by being 'open' for business 24 hours a day, 7 days a week and all without the capital cost of opening 'branches'. Or Canon, who listed the attributes of a photocopier: big, expensive, dirty, located in a basement somewhere, and then turned each rule on its head producing small, cheap, pastel-coloured photocopiers to sit in secretaries' offices.

Adjust your mind-set and, when enough people tell you the change you want to make is 'impossible', you are probably on the right track!

There are some marvellous techniques of creative thinking around which will help you and your team to see the world in new ways, for example: Edward de Bono's famous lateral thinking exercises, looking at problems in the form of pictures rather than words, using 'metaphors', brainstorming, scenario writing, day-dreaming. All these techniques help us challenge our mind-sets, make new connections and open ourselves up to the possibilities of change.

3.2   The change will change you

The classic adage is that change is something 'the top asks the middle to do to the bottom' (Rosabeth Moss Kanter). This assumes that the person who is 'doing' change can sit safely on the point of the organization pyramid orchestrating the process while those at the front line get changed. A fatal illusion. In making any change – personal or organizational – you risk yourself. As Tom Watson, founder of IBM, liked to say: 'The way to succeed is to double your failure rate.' A key emotional strength is not to be afraid of failure. There is a famous cartoon of Mikhail Gorbachev after his resignation. It shows him in his armchair with his finger near a nuclear button. An aide nearby explains, 'This button Mr G. now controls your TV set instead.' Gorbachev was never foolish enough to think that he controlled the change process in Russia or was immune from its effects, for as one of his Politburo colleagues observed at the time: 'He was like a coachman with a runaway cart.'

3.3   Believe you can make a difference

Management is not about preserving the status quo, but about creating the highest rate of change which the organization and its people can sustain. The essence of making change revolves around a very old-fashioned word: 'courage'. To paraphrase Saint Thomas Aquinas, 'the courage to change what has to be changed, the

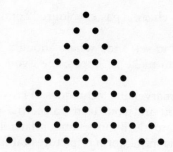

Figure 3.2 Only a dot in the organizational pyramid

tolerance to accept what can't be changed and the wisdom to know one from the other'. According to Dr Marshall Sashkin in his work on 'Visionary Leadership', effective leaders are characterized by a factor which he calls 'bottom-line leadership' – that is, the belief that you can make a difference. This behaviour comes from possessing a basic self-assurance that you can influence your own destiny and impact on people, events and organizational achievements.

It contrasts with the kind of passivity and helplessness which one frequently finds among the ranks of disillusioned middle management who have plateaued, feel they have few options open to them and have basically given up. They see themselves as powerless dots in the organization pyramid (see Figure 3.2), although, did they but know it, the movement of one dot can change the whole picture! As a professional change-maker, the manager wishing to make his mark on the organization will believe he can succeed. But at the same time, one of the great challenges of change is to convert attitudes of 'victimitis' in others into the attitude which says *I*, whoever I am, can make a difference around here.

3.4   The paradox of personal change

It's paradoxical but true that the person over whom you have most control is yourself but the hardest person to change is yourself. Like chastity, change is something which might be good for us but on the whole we'd rather it didn't happen just yet. In their work on managing change, Ashridge Management College sum this up beautifully (see Figure 3.3). Please add your own reasons/justifications!

Figure 3.3   For me to change I am waiting for . . .

Inspiration
Reassurance
My turn
The rest of the rules
Revenge
More time
The right person to appear
Time almost to run out
Mutual consent
A more favourable horoscope
The two-minute warning
Age to grant me the right of eccentricity
My annual check-up
Someone to discover me
A lower capital gains rate
The thing I do not understand or approve
of to go away
Someone to be watching
An end to poverty, injustice, cruelty,
deceit, incompetence, pestilence and
offensive suggestions from my peers
My subordinates to mature
The pot to boil
My self-esteem to be restored
The gems of brilliance buried within my
first bumbling efforts to be recognized,
applauded and substantially rewarded so
that I can work on the second draft in
comfort
The wind to freshen
My current life to be declared a dress
rehearsal, with some script changes
permitted before the opening night
The coffee to be ready
Someone else to change

A significant relationship to
(a) improve
(b) terminate
(c) happen
A disaster
An obvious scapegoat
The lion to lay down with the lamb
A better time
My youth to return
The legal profession to reform
Tomorrow
A better circle of friends
The Japanese to leave town
More adequate safeguards
A cure for herpes
A clearly written set of instructions
My new credit card
My suit to come back from the cleaners
A signal from heaven
Various aches and pains to subside
Someone else to screw up
My children to be thoughtful, neat,
obedient and self-supporting
Logic to prevail
A sharp pencil
My wife to come back
My smoking urges to subside
The rates to go up
My grandmother's estate to be settled
You to stand out of my light
A better deodorant
The cheque to clear
Permission
Someone to smooth the way
The stakes to be lower

Other reasons:

Source: Ashridge Management College

In any business organization, the behaviour of the manager who initiates a change will be closely watched to see if it is consistent with what he or she is saying. It's a case of putting your money where your mouth is, by signalling with your own behaviour that you can both 'walk' and 'talk' the change. If, for example, you are planning a major change programme to create customer focus or total quality, then you should ask yourself: 'What have I done today to help a customer?' It's not what you say, it's what you do from which your people will read the true message. If there is a mismatch between the two, they will draw their own conclusions about your commitment to the change. You are the ultimate role model. In change, actions speak louder than words.

How you choose to spend your time is always a powerful signal to the troops about what you really believe is important. Are you out with customers, communicating to employees, or sitting in the office doing paperwork? If you say you're trying to change the culture or management style, then are you prepared to demonstrate your commitment by attending every management training programme? Until quite recently, Marvin Bower, the founder/chairman of McKinsey Consultants, and then 85, turned up at every induction programme worldwide – a clear indication of how much weight he put on the indoctrination of new recruits into the firm.

3.5   Letting go

Change can only begin when one thing ends and something new starts. For this to happen we have to let go of the old, even though there can be no guarantee of what the new will bring. This can feel perilously like letting go of the only firm foothold and dangling off the cliff. Every instinct of human logic, survival and emotion argues against such an insanely risky course of action. Yet like abseiling, you actually do have to loosen your hold on the rope before you can start to move. Most of us have an understandable disinclination to give up any physical or emotional foothold we've spent time, money or effort acquiring. This seems to apply whether we're giving up power, possessions, people, habits, jobs, assumptions or even our own cherished self-image. Whatever one's trying to let go of has a funny habit of looking at its most desirable at that point. It's always hard to let go of the past, yet this is the necessary precursor for change. 'You have to let go' we say to the widow clinging to the memory of her lost husband, to the manager who refuses to relinquish power, to the mother learning to cope with an empty nest. They will nod in agreement with our collective wisdom, but doing something about it is very different.

Figure 3.4 poses the challenge: how good are you at letting go? Some managers give themselves high scores, pointing out that they feel very confident about moving house, job, country, even changing spouse. Others put themselves at the 'terrible' end of the spectrum, incapable of throwing out so much as an empty yoghurt carton and going into a form of grieving at every parting: end of

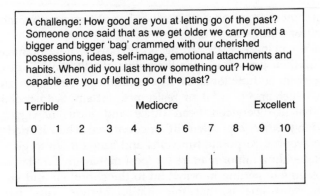

A challenge: How good are you at letting go of the past? Someone once said that as we get older we carry round a bigger and bigger 'bag' crammed with our cherished possessions, ideas, self-image, emotional attachments and habits. When did you last throw something out? How capable are you of letting go of the past?

Terrible				Mediocre					Excellent	
0	1	2	3	4	5	6	7	8	9	10

Figure 3.4 Letting go

holiday, move out of an office – even if they never liked it very much! It's easy to see which type of person copes with change best! Fortunately, most of us are somewhere in the middle, capable of letting go of some aspects of our life, providing continuity is retained in others. What is also obvious is that the more we have had previously successful change experiences the more likely we are to learn the confidence to let go of the past. Change can mean letting go of emotional attachments to people and ideas. Mikhail Gorbachev said that 'revolution means construction but it also always implies demolition, without demolition you cannot clear the site for new construction'. Yet when it came to making a sharp break with communism, he simply couldn't do it, until the *coup* in August 1990 did it for him. Throughout 1990 the British press was urging him on to break with communism and central authority with exhortations such as:

'Why is he hanging on to his party job?'
'The greatest worry is that whether from emotional attachment, fear of what party hardliners might do, or simple fear of the unknown, Mr Gorbachev is incapable of making a sharp enough break with the communist party.'
'Breaking with an organization he has worked so hard to reform would be painful.'

Mr Gorbachev was just like the rest of us in the strength of his emotional attachment – in his case to a party which had looked after him, which he believed in, which his parents had fought for. Yet fundamental change can only begin when there is an unambiguous divorce from the past.

Change can necessitate letting go of power. Few managers like giving up their powerbase and the habits of a lifetime. For example, moving from a functional to a decentralized structure can be a change which meets a lot of resistance. Attempts to redefine the power balance between head office and local managers rarely proceed smoothly, a problem BP encountered when it tried to slim down its central corporate functions and asked them to give up the habit of deciding minor matters for local managers. Similarly, one of the problems in getting information to the shopfloor and empowering the front line is that information systems are themselves political, vested interests are involved, you're changing information flow and that's threatening. In empowering the person in the job, the risk is that the supervisor or middle manager feels that he or she is being disempowered, and may hang on to their knowledge and powerbase like grim death.

Change can also mean letting go of a huge investment in the past. Gorbachev explained his own unwillingness to let go in words which apply equally to any individual or any corporation that is trying to change:

> Just think, how can we agree that 1917 was a mistake and all the 70 years of our life, work, effort and battles were also a complete mistake, that we were going in the wrong direction? – How does one accept that quite literally, 'the party's over'?

Change requires us to let go of the formula for past success. A Cranfield Business School professor quotes a company with which he was working on a business growth programme. The company itself had commissioned an analysis which would enable it to move from the 'where are we now?' to the 'where do we want to be?'. Their reaction to a fair but not uncritical report was: 'I don't think you understand how successful we've been.' And indeed, they had been successful and were very reluctant to give up their favourable self-image. Unfortunately, past success is no guarantee of corporate survival. Complacency about past success may well lie at the very heart of present problems.

Change means letting go of comfortable and familiar roles. Terry Cooke-Davies, owner/founder of two highly successful training consultancies, has a typical change dilemma. If his businesses are to exploit their potential he must redefine his role as the man who does everything. Comfort for him has been a full diary of client work.

Now he must let go of this comfort and free up his diary in order to find time to stand back from his business and develop his team, do less training himself and spend more time on consultancy with the top people of the corporations he deals with. He knows it makes sense, that he has to let go to move on, yet he catches himself wondering: 'Will I eat again?'

Sometimes change can mean letting go of one role before you can see the next. It is very useful to remind ourselves how difficult it is to let go of one role until we have found a viable alternative – a classic problem for the owner/founder of a growing business who must become less of a 'meddler'. But it is difficult to take your finger out of the pie unless you can find something equally satisfactory to do, perhaps as the 'strategist', the outward face of the company – a difficult transition. Or again the mother 'letting go' of her children; it's very difficult if she has no other role model for herself than that of 'mother'. One of the huge problems of the end of the Cold War has been what to do with half a million soldiers being sent home from shut-down military garrisons in Central and Eastern Europe. They will be giving up a lot, and for what? What will be their new role?

Learning to let go is essential if change is going to happen, but letting go means loss. Coping with loss is perhaps the greatest human challenge, one that none of us can avoid as countries, corporations, families or individuals. The only certainty over the next few years – apart from death and taxes – is that whatever worked in the past won't work in the future.

3.6 Managing personal transition

Before we look at transforming massive organizations, it may be salutary to remind ourselves of just how difficult it can be to achieve personal change. This way we may be able to stop doing unto others what we don't much like being done unto us. Most people, when initially asked for their views, will say that they like change, because this is what they think they are expected to say. Frequently, further discussion reveals that this simply is not true. As managers get in touch with their own pain in experiencing change, they usually adjust their original statement. If managers genuinely don't like change, then it is understandable but worrying. If they do like change it is almost more worrying, as the manager may assume that

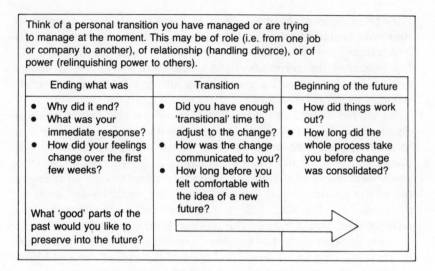

Figure 3.5   Making a personal transition

everyone else likes change just as much as he or she does and may therefore fail to put in place support mechanisms to manage the transition process. Generally, managers of maturity, who have suffered some setbacks in life, are more able to understand the process of change and the pain it can cause and can therefore be more sensitive in the way they handle those around them. To manage people effectively through change necessitates knowing the individual, not just as an economically viable unit of production, but as a whole person. This is the only way to avoid the cavalier approach of those to whom their staff are merely pieces to be pushed around the wargame board. Knowing others starts from 'know thyself'.

The exercise given in Figure 3.5 asks you to think back to your own experience of coping with a personal change, for example, a bereavement in the family or going away to school for the first time or a job change, redundancy or divorce. How did you feel? How long did it take you to acknowledge and achieve the change? What things helped or hindered you from doing so?

In any significant transition there is always something to be given up about which you will feel sad, bad or mad. There is always a more or less painful state of transition involving elements of discomfort, stress and fear as you move from the familiar past towards an unfamiliar future. Then there is always the dream of how things might be in the future which keeps you going through the whole ghastly process. It is identifying what these factors are, the balance between them, which will enable you to make the change.

Of course, the reality is that it takes time to get used to any change, perhaps longer than most of us admit. Think, for example, of how long people will struggle with a bad marriage, refusing to see the problems, refusing to move into the painful stage of ending what was. And yet this period of gestation, of working through, of the build-up over years of dissatisfaction, is essential if change is to happen.

Some of the factors which seem to help people move through the transition process are:

- Recognizing that something has ended and allowing yourself to grieve for its loss and preserve the good bits in your mind.

- Being given time to think about, 'hypothesize' a change, allowing yourself to imagine what it might be like before you are forced into a new situation.

- Consciously managing the in-between state as a transition, recognizing that sometimes you will move forward and sometimes you will regress and regret the past.

This model of transition seems to provide a useful framework for many kinds of personal changes and organizational change as, after all, the process is no different.

You may also want to map your pain levels over time as you experience the process of change. Usually pain levels are highest in the early stages as we move from accepting the end of the past into the transition phase. However, if insufficient information, support and time are given to adjust to change, then pain levels can maintain themselves at appallingly high levels for a very long time. On the chart shown in Figure 3.6 one manager in a major retail organization mapped a pain chart which was a straight line, at astronomic levels for a whole year, before he decided the only action for his survival was to leave that company.

It's clear that major change is likely to involve an increase in stress factors and that these need to be anticipated and managed. Work on stress levels suggests that the answer may be to ensure that if possible, we don't change too many things at the same time and maintain some point of continuity.

Let's take a look at Dr Richard Rahe's stress-related questionnaire (Figure 3.7). These life-events are all transitions and it's more than likely that you will have worked through quite a few of them,

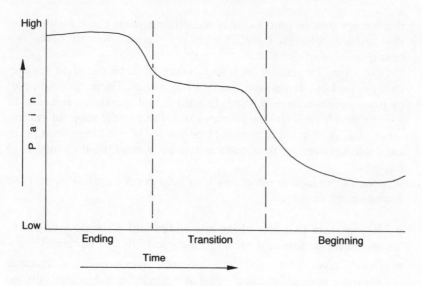

Figure 3.6 Mapping pain levels through the transition process (a typical graph)

though hopefully not too many all at once. Your score will give you a rough yardstick on the amount of stress you are currently experiencing.

Even when you are not experiencing any exceptionally stressful life-events, you are likely to have to handle the day-to-day stresses resulting from an ever-increasing rate of change. Change will always increase stress levels. Therefore, monitoring and coping with your own and others' stress levels becomes an important part of change management.

In their excellent book *Pressure at Work* Kim James and Tanya Arroba castigate us for what they describe as the 'John Wayne syndrome'. This consists of proudly wearing our badge of office and whatever extra demands are piled on us saying, 'I can cope.' That is until the point we crack, and all because we see it as a sign of weakness to admit that we are feeling dangerously pressured. People soon pick up the signals that only 'wimps' complain.

The problem is that stress is a very personal issue, one person's stress is another's motivation. This means that we all have to learn to take responsibility for monitoring our own stress levels. And it is worth the effort of doing so for once we have gone over our own optimum stress levels, we plunge very suddenly into a downward spiral from which it is difficult to claw our way back up. Better by far to realize we're on the edge and back off before it's too late.

Are you under stress? You can measure the amount of stress in your life using Dr Richard Rahe's stress scale. He has calculated the amount of stress that is caused by major life-events, and given each a numerical value. Have any of these events happened in your life in the last six months? If so, score for each that has occurred, then check the total to see if your life is overstressed.

Death of spouse/child	( )	10
Divorce	( )	8
Marital separation	( )	7
Jail term	( )	7
Death of a close family member	( )	7
Personal injury or illness	( )	6
Marriage	( )	6
Fired at work	( )	6
Marital reconciliation	( )	5
Retirement	( )	5
Change of health of family member	( )	5
Pregnancy	( )	5
Sex difficulties	( )	4
Gain of new family member	( )	4
Business readjustment	( )	4
Change in financial state	( )	4
Death of a close friend	( )	4
Change to a different line of work	( )	4
A large mortgage loan	( )	4
Foreclosure of mortgage or loan	( )	4
Change in responsibilities at work	( )	3
Son or daughter leaving home	( )	3
Trouble with in-laws	( )	3
Outstanding personal achievement	( )	3
Spouse begins or stops work	( )	3
Begin or end school or college	( )	3
Change in living conditions	( )	3
A change in personal habits	( )	3
Trouble with the boss	( )	3
Change in work hours or conditions	( )	3
Change in residence	( )	2
Change in school or college	( )	2
Change in recreation	( )	2
Change in social activities	( )	2
Change in eating habits	( )	2
Holiday	( )	2
Christmas	( )	2
Minor violations of law	( )	2

How to score:

Below 6:	Your life has been unusually free from stress lately.
6 to 8:	You have had a normal amount of stress recently. This score is average for the ordinary wear and tear of life.
8 to 10:	The stress in your life is a little high, probably because of one recent event.
10 upwards:	Pressures are piling up, either at home or work, or both. You are under serious stress and the higher you score above 10 the worse the strain.

Note: It is calculated that people scoring over 30 run the risk of developing a major illness in the next two years.

Source: T. Holmes and R. Rahe. Reprinted with permission from Pergamon Press Ltd, Oxford, England

Figure 3.7 The social readjustment rating scale

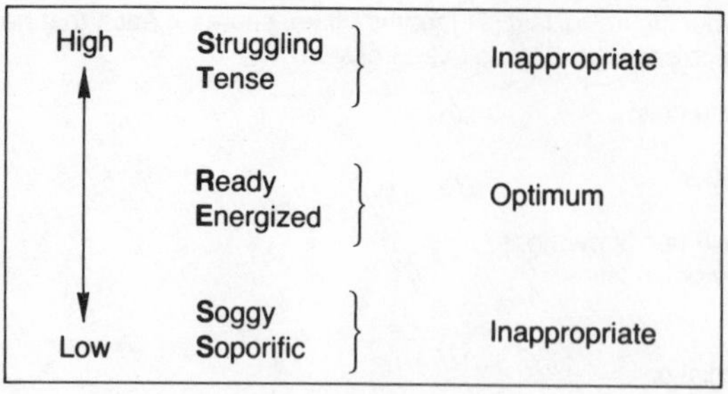

Source: James and Arroba, 'Pressure at work', 1992. Reproduced with permission of McGraw-Hill

Figure 3.8 Stress levels

Stress, as Kim explains, is the twentieth century's equivalent of the caveman's 'fight or flight' responses to encountering woolly mammoths. Attention leads to action, the threat goes away and we then relax. The problem starts when we never switch off, but are in a state of constant alert for woolly mammoths, real or imagined. Then we're going to need to recognize the signs both in ourselves and others, for example, mental or emotional or physical or behavioural changes, and either reduce unnecessary pressures or increase our buoyancy and resistance. If we or our teams remain highly stressed over long periods of time, then we jeopardize our chance of sustaining change.

3.7   From meddler to strategist: influencing styles

The nature of your behaviour and your relationship with your management team is, according to a recent Cranfield Business School survey, a determining factor in managing change and realizing business growth potential. The researchers noted two key elements of this relationship: first, the amount of time spent on routine management tasks such as marketing, selling, analyzing figures and reviewing budgets. A high score on the vertical axis indicates that the manager is still largely preoccupied with the day-to-day business and may have difficulty in letting go. The second factor, examined on the horizontal axis, looks at the quality and business skills of the management team in total. Here a low

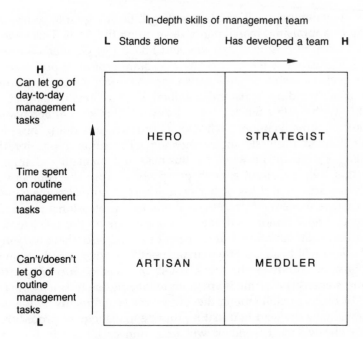

Figure 3.9   From meddler to strategist

score would be a new, untrained or unconfident and dependent team, a high score would be a high calibre, in-depth management team.

We are all inevitably a bit of everything and sometimes one style is more appropriate at certain phases of growth and to deal with particular business issues. However, it is important to examine how you personally strike the balance: your natural positioning between the four style labels of ARTISAN, HERO, MEDDLER and STRATEGIST. Please complete the questionnaire at the end of this chapter (p. 64), you will then be able to plot your scores on the histogram.

Let's briefly examine the characteristic behaviours which underlie each style 'label'.

The *artisan* is typified by low occupation with routine manage-ment tasks, because most of the time is spent producing a product or selling a service. The level of business skills and the depth of the management resource is also low because most people are employed in production or carrying out primary tasks such as book-keeping or selling. The owner/founder is still very much 'one of the gang', passionately committed to the product and the customer and

revenue-generating activities but putting little energy into communicating or appraising, managing or developing the team. This style is
quite typical of business start-ups and Phase 1 of Greiner's 'growth
through creativity'. It's apparently also quite typical of professional
firms such as architects and surveyors, manufacturers, subcontrac-
tors, small building firms and members of small retail chains. One
might say that Clive Sinclair tended towards this kind of behaviour,
far keener on invention, technology, product and doing his own
thing than in professional management. The implications for the
artisan's success in growing the business and managing change is
that this style will limit growth prospects because the company is
really the artisan and his or her craft. There is no real management
team nor management process. Sometimes a professional manager,
no matter how senior, is dragged into this box by the need to sort
out a particular situation, but it doesn't pay to linger there too long.

The *hero* will head up one management function, or a division of
the business. Indeed the hero could be heading up the entire
business enterprise. Time is spent on managing the business. As the
level of business skill among the employees is still relatively low the
hero will take the lead in initiating routine management procedures.
He or she will be trained or will train him or herself in business
techniques, will get the ideas and will introduce them to the firm.
Though these will be communicated well and fluently, the hero will
be the only person who really understands what's going on. The
managerially inexperienced team will consequently see this person
as the hero.

The hero can occur at any stage of Greiner's growth curve, but
emerges particularly at times of 'revolution' and crisis. We all love a
hero, someone who is readily identifiable, larger than life, a big ego
perhaps, but a big man or woman behind it. Or so goes the
mythology. Unfortunately, the hero has a herculean task on his or
her hands. By continually solving all the business problems, and
making all the decisions, the hero creates dependency. Then when
the business gets bigger and the landscape more complex he or she
cannot shed the 'doing' tasks because there is no one with any
capability to take them on. The management team has never been
trained to make decisions for itself. The hero has a high capacity
for improving the performance of the firm because of his or her
strength, motivation, direction and management skill, *but* the hero
still has low growth prospects relative to the market. There is no
time for strategic thinking and no depth of management to handle
change effectively. The hero who cannot grow other heroes can
become a menace if not a meddler.

At this moment one large and famous British company is recovering from the ejection of its powerful but paranoid chairman. The new man chosen by the City is more of a strategist than a hero, but in the early days of the transition the top management team are running round like headless chickens. They've been told to get on and run their part of the business but they haven't yet got their hands on the paperwork describing the decisions of the past – they're all filed in the outgoing chairman's office. Richard Branson is another example of a hero who is very consciously moving himself into the strategist box by realizing that activities such as hot air ballooning are no longer appropriate for a chairman who has to develop strategy and resource within the notoriously competitive industry of airlines.

The *meddler* raises the level of management skill either by training or recruitment, but then cannot let go of routine management tasks. The meddler is typical of Phase 2 'growth through direction' when much time is spent introducing more refined but often unnecessary management systems and also of Phase 4 big company behaviour when having delegated some responsibility he or she may spend a lot of time cross-checking and second-guessing to maintain control and stop things going wrong. The meddler also goes on courses or reads books to become even more knowledgeable and sometimes better at routine management than subordinates, who anyway are by now doing a perfectly satisfactory job of managing today's business. The meddler gets in early and leaves late. The meddler's problem is an ability to let go of routine management tasks because the day will feel empty. He or she has been used to a 70–90-hour week with only ten days' holiday a year. Once the management team is in place and trained, the meddler's out of a job. Until he or she reduces his or her involvement with routine management tasks he or she will limit the capacity of the business to change, for two reasons. First, the management team won't make new changes if the changes are the meddler's not theirs and the reward for taking on the last lot was being nagged and criticized. Second, the meddler is too busy checking on people to develop sound change strategies for growth.

The *strategist* has the most desirable style for managing change and growing the business. He or she is truly a change master – the 'visionary' who creates the dream, the magnet which keeps the business moving forward and constantly motivates and empowers people. One thinks of Anita Roddick of Body Shop or Jim Treybig of Tandem Computers. The strategist develops the management skills of his team to the highest appropriate level and in depth. This will free up his or her time and the time of the key managers to think strategically. The strategist will devote roughly a third of his or her time to management tasks such as monitoring performance, resolving conflict, co-ordinating activities, a third to motivating, counselling and developing the management team and a third to strategic thinking for tomorrow's business.

The natural path of development for the manager as his business gets older and bigger and grows up the Greiner growth curve is to pass from artisan to hero to meddler and for the lucky few on to strategist. By examining the balance of your score, you will get some clues on whether you are a hero who needs to move a bit more towards strategist (a touch less John Wayne, a touch more Hanson), whether you have the tendency to become a meddler and should encourage yourself to 'let go' and grow, or whether you're basically an artisan, immersed in the technology and believing that if you want a job doing do it yourself. Good luck with your personal journey of change!

EXERCISE 3

CHALLENGING YOUR ASSUMPTIONS AND THE STRATEGIST QUESTIONNAIRE

Part 1: 'Paradigm Lost'

We all view the world through a lens made up of our personal prejudices and deeply held assumptions and beliefs. Not all of these are entirely rational or appropriate but at least in recognizing them we may eliminate some potential barriers to change. Do you recognize any of the following to do with your:

1. Personal prejudices?
2. Business assumptions?
3. Underlying values?

1. *Personal prejudices*
Most of us make up our minds about someone on the basis of minimal and potentially misleading cues to do with appearance, dress, accent, and we do it in 30 seconds flat. Do you dislike any of the following?

Scotsmen	People with limp handshakes
Americans	Sandals worn with socks
Fat people	Button-down collars
Women in business	Men with long hair
Birmingham accents	Scruffy people
People who know more than you do	Small men

2. *Business assumptions*
Please put a √ for Yes and a X for No

1. If I conform and don't challenge the status quo I'll get to the top ☐
2. The people I manage aren't looking for the same motivation as myself ☐
3. If in doubt, I tell them how much more than themselves I'm earning ☐
4. ⁻/ly abilities will never become inappropriate to this organization ☐
5. I'll never be unemployed, divorced or bankrupt ☐
6. I'm as 'green' as I'm ever going to be ☐
7. Business should offer a job for life ☐
8. Technology change won't affect how my business operates ☐
9. I can afford to ignore this thing called 'Europe' ☐
10. There's no such thing as the unexpected competitor ☐
11. I'm in a static market ☐
12. Of course, the job I'm doing has to be done ☐
13. A productive employee is an employee I can see ☐
14. I've got the right balance between 'hard' business issues and 'soft' people issues ☐
15. Hierarchy and structure are the key to motivating, promoting and rewarding people ☐

Like too many units of alcohol consumption, if you have *even one* tick, then your consumption of comfortable illusions may seriously damage your health.

3. *Underlying values*
What relative importance would you place on the following items as they affect your business life?

Core Values		High		Moderate		Low
		1	2	3	4	5
Security:	'I want to be safe'					
Money:	'I want to be seriously rich'					
Power:	I want to be in charge'					
Recognition:	'I want to be rated'					
Technical competence:	'I want to be the expert'					
General management:	'I want to grow people'					
Independence or autonomy:	'I want to want alone'					
Entrepreneur:	'I want to build a business'					
Affiliative:	'I want to be loved'					
Achievement:	'I want the challenge'					
Family:	'I want to spend time with the family'					
Dedication to service:	'I want to make a difference in the world'					

Part 2: The strategist questionnaire
Complete this questionnaire to find out if you are a strategist, a hero or simply a meddler when it comes to managing your business.

Instructions for Completion
1. Complete the questionnaire, scoring each question 1 for agree and 0 for disagree.
2. Transfer your completed scores to the profile grid.
3. Total each column of the profile grid.
4. Plot you personal histogram using the profile scores from the grid.

Q1 I don't believe in asking anyone to do a job I can't do myself. ☐
Q2 Sod's law says that if things can go wrong, they will go wrong. I'm here to keep my finger on the pulse. ☐
Q3 I've managed to free up my time so that I can spend almost two days a week on engineering tomorrow rather than managing today. ☐
Q4 Few people would be in any doubt that I'm the boss. ☐

Q5 I live, eat and breathe the job 24 hours a day. My wife and family would probably say they suffer. ☐

Q6 I believe in a high and continuous investment in appraising, training and developing the management team. ☐

Q7 I'm quite happy to roll up my sleeves and get stuck in. ☐

Q8 Sometimes the only way to get something to happen is to do it yourself. ☐

Q9 I place a high reliance on regular downward briefings. ☐

Q10 I try to spend as little time as possible on the day-to-day management processes. ☐

Q11 I would bet that 10–20 potential crises hit my desk each day. My job is to solve them before they explode. ☐

Q12 I'm usually the first person in the office and the last to leave in the evening. I rarely take holidays longer than one week. ☐

Q13 I communicate primarily by setting the vision of where we're going and the values or 'way we do things around here'. I'm not interested in the detail. ☐

Q14 My job is to make the decisions around here, and I do. ☐

Q15 I don't believe in creating distance. I'm very much one of the gang. ☐

Q16 I probably spend 75 per cent of my time on routine management tasks, particularly checking and cross-checking that things get done. ☐

Q17 Although I try to 'walk the job' my primary internal role is to resource my immediate management team. ☐

Q18 I don't think anyone would complain of lack of direction from me. ☐

Q19 I believe in a hands-on style of management. ☐

Q20 My primary role is to ensure our day-to-day revenue and make sure that every hour that can be sold is sold. ☐

Q21 I believe one year ahead is about as long term as one can realistically get. ☐

Q22 I spend approximately one third of my time on routine management tasks, about one third motivating, counselling and developing my managers and one third on the future of the business. ☐

Q23 I tend to rely on 1-to-1 communications and the written word. I scan all the post, write lots of memos and always check the agendas of meetings. ☐

Q24 I like the whole technology of what we're doing. The product is intrinsically interesting. ☐

Q25 I need to be respected first, admired second, hated third and ignored fourth. ☐

Q26 I'd like to be remembered through the business and people I've grown. I don't need to be famous. ☐

Q27 I personally deal with irate or dissatisfied customers. ☐

Q28 My skills come to the fore in times of corporate turn-round and crisis. I can pull the rabbit out of the hat when needed. ☐

Q29 I take pride in a job well done, that we produce the product and deliver a service. ☐

Q30 I have to keep control of a huge mass of detail. There's little time to worry about strategic development tomorrow. ☐

Q31 Asked whether I'm the greatest, most people would say: 'We did it ourselves.' ☐

Q32 Because my management team is inexperienced I generally find that where I lead others follow. ☐☐

Q33 I rely on informal communications on an *ad hoc* basis.

Q34 I'm spending a lot of time introducing and fine-tuning management systems to do with operating procedures and people procedures. ☐☐

Q35 I'm trying to make a new business for tomorrow.

Q36 Most of our people are concerned with getting product out, or tasks such as book-keeping and selling. ☐

Q37 I spend a lot of my time on personal business training programmes, making external presentations, etc. I'm known in the industry, and they do tend to ask for me rather than any of my staff. ☐

Q38 I've made a big investment in trying to train my team and drag them kicking and screaming into new ways. ☐

Q39 Turning managerial 'mice' into 'men' is one of the challenges I most enjoy. ☐☐

Q40 Survival today is the name of the game.

Profile grid

Q1	Q4	Q2	Q3
Q7	Q9	Q5	Q6
Q8	Q11	Q12	Q10
Q15	Q14	Q16	Q13
Q20	Q18	Q19	Q17
Q24	Q21	Q23	Q22
Q29	Q25	Q27	Q26
Q33	Q28	Q30	Q31
Q36	Q32	Q34	Q35
Q40	Q37	Q38	Q39
Total A	H	M	S

Please transfer your scores from the profile grid and plot your personal histogram.

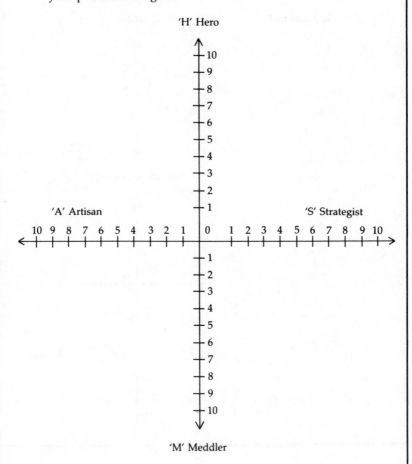

'H' Hero

'A' Artisan

'S' Strategist

'M' Meddler

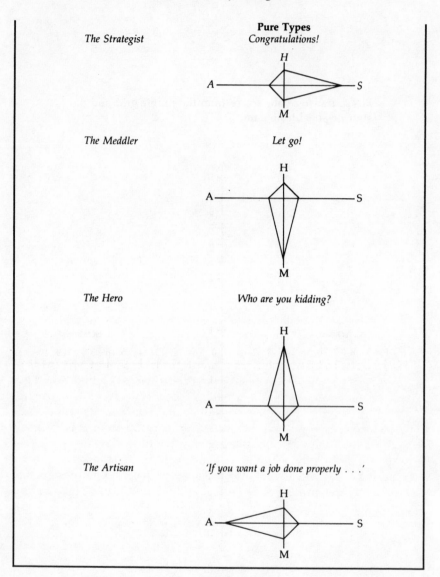

Pure Types

The Strategist — *Congratulations!*

The Meddler — *Let go!*

The Hero — *Who are you kidding?*

The Artisan — *'If you want a job done properly . . .'*

3.8   Summary

Change won't go away. There isn't a fault in reality so the only thing we can adjust is our personal mind-set. You are the X factor in managing and surviving change successfully. As business para-

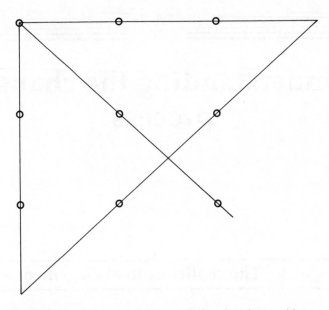

Figure 3.10 At least one answer to the nine dots problem

digms shift so fast, you may want to take the opportunity to challenge the appropriateness of your personal assumptions and get out of the box of routine thinking. Leaders of change are not themselves immune to the effects of change, the change will change you. In the end the only person you can really change is yourself and yet you are probably the hardest person to change! The best way of helping others through change is to understand emotionally as well as intellectually what it feels like to make a painful personal transition, the problems of letting go and the issues surrounding becoming a strategist and not a meddler.

4

Understanding the change process

4.1 The challenge to management

This and the next chapter address the issues of understanding and spreading experience of the change process and increasing the receptiveness of the organization as a 'culture' which will allow change to take root. We will share some of the learnings from major programmes of change within companies such as ICL and introduce and discuss models which get at the essence of the change process, and which start to give us all a language of change. Just as the Inuit are supposed to have more than 20 words for snow, reflecting its importance to them, so the more we can get people talking about change, the more we will increase awareness of and sensitivity in dealing with the issues involved.

Even the routine, day-to-day changes inherent in running any business, such as introducing new products, new faces or new systems, are frequently accompanied by political intrigue, squabbles, tension, stress, foot dragging and sabotage – in other words, by resistance. If this is the case with small changes, imagine how much more difficult it is to get big changes to happen, for example, major programmes of culture change, restructuring the business or divesting and merging companies.

We have only to observe people in a meeting or the staff canteen or relaxing in the pub to know that the human being is a creature of habit who likes familiar patterns: the same table, the same group of friends to talk to over lunch. Most of us don't like change, we like things to stay the same. Yet the pace of change and the pressures from the external social, economic and political environment are forcing change, whether we like it or not.

Here lies the dilemma for management. Making people feel good about change is the challenge. The most common error in organizations is to underestimate the impact of change on people. It is an extraordinarily expensive error as it increases the probability that the change will fail, sends pain levels sky high and disrupts day-to-day productivity. Yet managers continue to demonstrate an astonishing lack of sensitivity in the way they handle change.

Part of developing this sensitivity is to understand the nature of the change process and the predictable phases or steps of change so that the manager can prepare and reassure people about what is happening. Managing change is no different in this respect from coping with a stroke or developing a good golf swing: the more you know about the process you're going through the more you can manage yourself and support others. Giving as many people in the business as possible an understanding of the process of change means creating a shared vocabulary, legitimizing the hurt and discomfort people will feel, letting them know what to expect and helping to create a feeling that 'we're all in it together'.

There is, in fact, no significant difference between organizational change and personal change. The process is identical. It's a pity that more managers do not apply to business life the painful learnings they have acquired in coping with personal changes, such as bereavement, divorce or job loss. Change always involves loss – loss of the past, loss of routine, loss of comfort, loss of relationships. But it can also be the start of something new, if we allow it to be. Even unwelcome change can precipitate great opportunities for growth. This chapter will develop three major findings: first, that change hurts; second, that it is a predictable process and can therefore be managed; and third, that understanding inevitable sources of resistance will help managers convert negatives into positives.

4.2 Change hurts

More of the same, repeating the formula of past success, comes naturally, we need predictability, routine, familiar patterns to survive at all. We strive to preserve the status quo at all costs – after all, that's what got us where we are. Change, therefore, threatens us in the head, heart and guts. The analogy of the 'change castle'

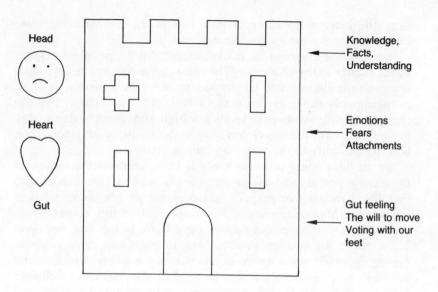

Figure 4.1   Storming the change castle

(shown in Figure 4.1) is a nice one: our security and identity are being stormed at many levels.

There is a strange mythology around which encourages us to believe that while in 'real' life most of us are quite emotional beings, once we get into a business environment we become entirely rational and logical. The change castle suggests that nothing is further from the truth. Managing change isn't just a cerebral process of getting across the 'facts' of the situation. Frequently when faced with change, people will nod their heads, but their feet still won't move. This is because we haven't got to grips with the fears, doubts and gut feeling of those involved. Until we do, nothing is going to happen. As Edgar Schein, Professor of Management at the MIT Sloan School of Management explains, learning is too often thought of purely as knowledge acquisition and gaining skills, but it is emotional conditioning which is actually the third and most power-ful type of learning in organizations. Put a dog in a green room, says Schein, ring a bell and give the dog a painful electric shock. It will learn to cower at the sound of the bell and to avoid the room. Even after the shock mechanism has been turned off, the dog will never enter the room and so will never find out that it isn't in danger (Schein, 1993).

Any proposed change can be perceived as a bell signifying that we are about to jump into a scary green room. Change always raises anxiety levels and encourages avoidance behaviour, particularly when the new change runs against all the accumulation of prior learning based on prior success. Hence the 'victim' behaviour which so often characterizes organizations: no we can't say what we think, challenge, take stock, be empowered because someone will punish us!

Resistance to change is the natural reaction. It is also not as unreasonable as many managers think. Just as sales objections are inevitable in the sales process, to be anticipated and even encouraged as a sign of interest, so resistance to change is unavoidable and can even be harnessed as part of the momentum for change. Many of the sources of resistance intellectually, emotionally and at a gut level are extremely sensible in the face of the unknown and the unknowable. After all, the perceived threat may be a real one. Change usually produces winners and losers, and individuals in the latter case may well be about to lose much in the way of security, status or clout.

Work with managerial groups shows that change is Janus-faced, the two sides representing both threat and opportunity. Change always involves negatives but it can have tremendous positives too. However, it has to be said that most groups identify far more negatives than positives, often in the proportion of 80:20.

The 'negatives' given in Figure 4.2 (overleaf) are typical reactions to change. Some of them we have already talked about, others give an interesting new slant, for example, 'resentment'. Most individuals join an organization with a 'psychological contract' in mind: 'I will give X and you will deliver Y.' Unfortunately, the external pressures on organizations mean that these rules can be unilaterally changed and the implied contract between individual and organization shifted, causing understandable resentment. This often happens with middle managers who have been with a company a long time and have very entrenched expectations about their job security, status and comfort levels, only to find that after twenty years of fighting their way up the managerial ladder the rules have been changed.

One organization we know is contemplating banning smoking altogether (at present there are smoking rooms). What about the heavy smoker who joined you when lifestyles were different? Isn't his contract being infringed?

Another interesting negative reaction to change is 'loss of peer group network'. Breaking up teams and ripping the sinews of

+ Positives	− Negatives
Enthusiasm	Fear
Opportunity	Anxiety
Challenge	Shock
Excitement	Distrust
New skills	Anger
New knowledge	Stress
Reward	Resentment
Fulfilment	Confusion/disorientation
Survival	Uncertainty
New start	Demotivation
Creates options	Depression
Learning experience	Loss of self-esteem
Motivation	Loss of identity
	Loss of peer group network
	Letting go
	Saying goodbye
	Poor health
	Distraction
	Family disruption
	Insomnia
	Conflict
	Politics
	Stubborness
	Critical reactions
	Mutiny
	High risk
	Disown/block out
	Resistance
	Misunderstanding
	Personality change

Figure 4.2 How individuals typically react to change

established relationships is always a danger signal for change. Tracy Kidder, in his marvellous book *Soul of a New Machine*, talks about the creation of the 'Eclipse' machine in the United States and the passionate and emotional outcry which followed the disbanding of the original project team who had lived, worked and breathed the project for so long.

But there are positives too. Change can put a charge in the air, like the ionization effect after a thunderstorm. Change means opportunity, options and excitement. The trick for the manager is to work on people's perceptions of change so that they see more of the positives and fewer of the negatives.

The people costs of change can also hit organizations very hard. ICL, now aligned with Fujitsu, has gone from strength to strength, and has certainly become a master of change management in a very tough industry. We will explore in Chapter 5 how culture for change. But it was not always so.

ICL in the early 1980s: change hurts

In the early 1980s ICL, the only remaining computer manufacturer in the United Kingdom, was struggling for survival. Few people would have bet their shirts on the outcome. In 1983 ICL was rescued from the brink of disaster by a combined City and government deal, and Sir Michael Edwardes was put in as chairman. Of his earlier experience in BL he had written: 'It is easier to lead a defence of the status quo than to lead people into something new with all the attendant uncertainties and the innate fear of the unknown which change implies.'

The ICL culture in 1982 was resistant to change. So much so that when the chairman pulled hard on the lever for change, nothing happened. This represented a sizeable problem of organizational inertia, which jarred harshly with ICL's need to respond fast or go out of business.

Even the metaphors used by managers at the time demonstrate how punitive the culture was. People talked about 'keeping your head below the parapets' or of 'tap dancing your way out of trouble'. Figure 4.3 shows a selection of management comments from an attitude survey in 1983, which contrast strikingly with a shrewd observation from the then chairman, Sir Michael Edwardes.

In this kind of environment people did not feel safe. There were more losers than winners around, and without conditions of psychological safety there were few opportunities to practise and make errors, let alone for error detection! Avoidance behaviour learnt through punishment is very stable. People will learn to limit themselves to safe ranges or become paralyzed with fear. To speed up the kind of learning necessary for real change we need to provide a supportive environment characterized by encouragement, opportunities for training, coaching and rewards, achievable targets, praise and freedom to experiment and make mistakes. People who feel unsafe retrench.

Thus, even while the managing director, Robb Wilmot, was announcing that 'every part of our business has changed, is changing and will continue to change', people within ICL perceived change as a temporary and unnecessary disruption of the status quo. They believed that once management got it 'right', change would go away and their lives could get back to normal. They didn't really want to see how inevitable change was for ICL's survival; the personal cost and effort of doing so was too great.

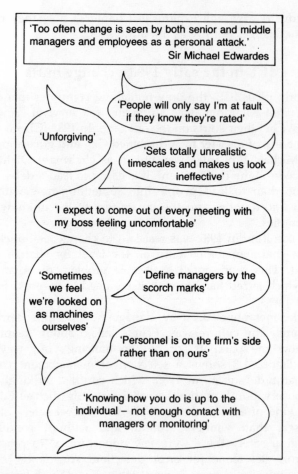

'Too often change is seen by both senior and middle managers and employees as a personal attack.'
Sir Michael Edwardes

'People will only say I'm at fault if they know they're rated'

'Unforgiving'

'Sets totally unrealistic timescales and makes us look ineffective'

'I expect to come out of every meeting with my boss feeling uncomfortable'

'Sometimes we feel we're looked on as machines ourselves'

'Define managers by the scorch marks'

'Personnel is on the firm's side rather than on ours'

'Knowing how you do is up to the individual – not enough contact with managers or monitoring'

Figure 4.3 ICL in the early 1980s: a culture for change?

So change has productivity costs but it also has people costs. Change 'hurts'. Figure 4.4 lists some comments from ICL from the 1983/4 period.

It is interesting that these comments arose, not from 'feely-touchy' people in the personnel department but from middle and senior managers with solid scientific and managerial backgrounds and frequently double PhDs in esoteric subjects. Yet their reaction to change was emotional and visceral, rather than cerebral. The comments on stress levels were particularly important, with absenteeism then running at twice the levels of the Thames Valley norms and many managers showing all the physical signs of

---

Fear

- 'Don't think the company realize how frightened people are.'

Loss

- 'Teams broken, relationships broken, lack of commitment to keeping our unit.'

Discomfort

- 'We feel very battered.'

Stress

- Personal overloads
  'In the past we worked hard and played hard and people laughed – they don't anymore.'

Figure 4.4   Change hurts

extreme discomfort. The place was full of unsmiling faces, sweaty bodies and the smell of fear.

4.3   The predictable process of change

If it is possible to predict the stages which people go through in reacting to a significant organizational or personal change, then it is possible to help manage them through the process. But the process of change is never linear. It is messy and iterative, it goes in fits and starts as one lets go of the past, copes with the transition stage and contemplates the new future.

The Beckhard and Harris model (Figure 4.5, overleaf) replicates at an organizational level the same approach we used in Chapter 3 in looking at letting go and coping with difficult personal transitions. Put another way, the three questions:

Where have we been?

Where are we now?

Where are we going?

are the bedrock of all organization change. As we'll see in later chapters, if you do no more than share this model with your management team, posing the three questions and encouraging them to brainstorm characteristics of past, present and future, then you will have made a great start in spreading awareness of the change process.

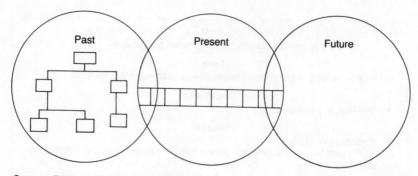

Source: Richard Beckhard and Reuben T. Harris (1987), reprinted by permission of Addison Wesley

Figure 4.5 Organization transition

It's easy to see how difficult change is to 'fix' and how easy it is to regress to the safe and familiar past. In Chapter 1 we talked about ICI's demerger as a response to external pressure. Arguably without Lord Hanson's threatened takeover, ICI would never have summoned the courage to make the change. It was interesting that before ICI truly got the message, the press in the early 1990s was commenting that although briefly energized by Lord Hanson's prodding, it looked as though once that immediate threat had been removed, the Board would regress to status quo behaviour. Individuals coping with major change oscillate between the tugs of the past and the vision of the new future. This whole process is described in Figure 4.6.

The 'unfreeze–change–refreeze' model sums up very simply a lot of the complex issues which underlie letting go of the past and sustaining change in the long term. For an organization to change, it must be destabilized or unfrozen. It must be converted from a 'solid' to a 'liquid' state. That is why change is always fluid, messy, ambiguous. The very ambiguity is the characteristic which gives the propensity for movement and change. To speed up learning we must speed up the unfreezing process. If change always involves

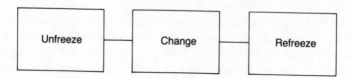

Figure 4.6 Unfreeze–change–refreeze model

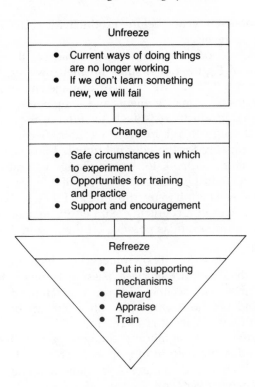

Figure 4.7 Learning to change

anxiety, then 'unfreezing' means creating an even greater anxiety around the perception that the current ways are no longer working and that if people don't learn something new, they will fail. The process is not dissimilar to the 'brainwashing' associated with all ideologies. As Figure 4.7 indicates, 'unfreezing' creates the momentum for change and is a step in the process which cannot be neglected. The 'change' or transition state by contrast is a state where people need the conditions of psychological safety, support and coaching, while they struggle with new risks and new ambiguities. 'Refreezing' means using the infrastructure of systems, procedures, structures and job responsibilities which ensure that people cannot regress and that the change is truly bedded down.

Almost any major change will make things worse before it makes them better. The reality of the productivity curve means that the immediate impact of change is a decrease in productivity as people struggle with new ways of doing things, cope with their own learning curve and desperately try to 'keep the shop open'. It may be months or even years before productivity recovers, let alone exceeds original levels.

Most managers nod in agreement when they see the 'productivity curve' shown in Figure 4.8. It sums up their own experience. The lessons are several: first, we need to manage the expectations of shareholders, senior management and employees so that they understand that productivity is likely to suffer in the short term and that getting through this 'blip' will take time. Second, we need to have some sympathy for the poor beleaguered people charged with making the change happen, for whom change will mean they have all the old demands plus, running in parallel, a lot of new ones. Their 'buckets' will be full to overflowing and they will need support from their manager in recognizing extra effort, managing stress and keeping as much pressure as possible off them from those higher in the organization.

The change process has its own lifecycle, which might almost be compared with a product lifecycle passing through the stages of growth, maturity and decline and also characterized by the early innovators and by those who will only climb on board with the change when they can see it is successful!

In responding to a significant change, people themselves go through a predictable pattern of response. This has been described as the 'transition curve' (Figure 4.9), illustrating an individual's response to change over time.

It is interesting that at the beginning of the change transition self-esteem may rise. Perhaps this is to do with the initial euphoria, the 'halo' effect which can surround the announcement of a change, the 'buzz' before the reality sinks in. For example, one manager recently described his reactions to a desired change as follows: 'I had been really looking forward to the prospect of promotion. Eventually the telephone call came through. I was ecstatic, floating on a cloud. Then I put the phone down and said to myself "Oh my God".' Depression tends to set in as the reality of what is involved starts to dawn. Even a 'good' change will involve extra effort, fear of failure, new learnings. With letting go comes acceptance of the change, and from this point on real change starts to happen as we experiment with new behaviours and internalize those that seem to work.

In Figure 4.10 Fink, Beak and Taddeo describe a four-stage process through which people typically pass in learning to adjust to a personal change such as bereavement or an organization change such as a relocation, redundancy or restructuring.

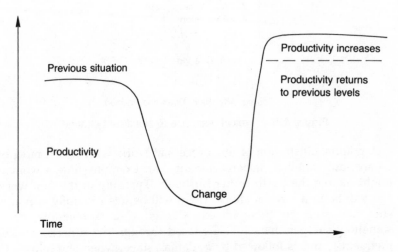

Figure 4.8 The productivity curve

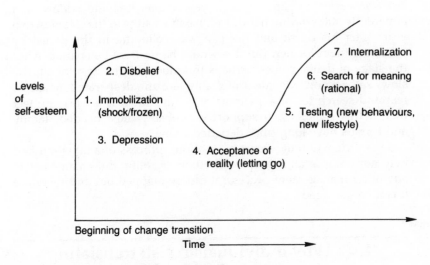

Source: Based on Adams, Hayes and Hopson (1976)

Figure 4.9 Self-esteem changes during transitions

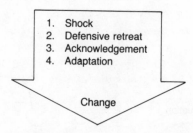

1. Shock
2. Defensive retreat
3. Acknowledgement
4. Adaptation

Change

Source: After Fink, Beak and Taddeo

Figure 4.10 Typical response to significant change

A graphic illustration of this process at work, with which most of us are sadly familiar, is bereavement – for example, how a woman might handle the death of her husband. Typically in the first week she will be in a state of shock, there will be lots of family support, she may well be tranquillized, she is in a zombie-like state, somehow she gets herself white-faced through the funeral service. Frequently, this is followed by a 'denial' stage, when she refuses to acknowledge that this unwelcome change has in fact occurred and is irreversible. She may retreat into a fantasy world where she expects to hear her husband's key in the door at any moment. This stage can last for weeks, months or even years. One grieving widow was apparently still sending her dead husband's suits to the cleaners two years after his death and her son was colluding in the denial by collecting them for her. But this would be unusual behaviour. After the stage of denial comes perhaps the most painful stage of all, the slow, sad acknowledgement of reality and the desperate loneliness, fear and search for new patterns of behaviour. It is a worrying fact that at this stage, when support is probably most needed, family and friends have long since departed home.

So real change only occurs after a long process of adaptation and may not occur at all if people get stuck en route. But change is like any other management process; it can be mapped out and therefore it can be managed.

4.4 Why individuals resist: translating negatives into positives

---

Key to translating the negatives of change into positives is the manager's ability to expect resistance and to analyze the reasons why individuals and teams tend to resist change. Pinpointing the source of resistance makes it possible to see what needs to be done and to present change in such a way that there is a better chance of its being perceived as opportunity rather than threat. Work with management groups indicates that there are perhaps seven major factors in resistance to organization change, and therefore seven 'clues' for management action. These are:

1. Loss of control.
2. Why are you doing it?
3. Uncertainty and ambiguity.
4. Springing surprises.
5. Loss of face.
6. Can I cope?
7. More work.

4.4.1 Loss of control

The biggest concern which most people in organizations have about change is that it is something which is done to them rather than by them. Most of us want and need to feel in control of events around us; it's a question of choice and ownership. The more change is imposed from the outside the more it will be resisted, and the more it will be seen as a threatening rather than an exciting change. As Rosabeth Moss Kanter says: 'it is powerlessness which corrupts, not power.' The more that we make people feel victims of change, the more they will rally their defences to sabotage it. People who are powerless become terrified, negative, apathetic. They feel they have no control over their own destiny, therefore on principle they will resist. 'Empowerment' is the flavour of the moment and yet all too few people in businesses really do feel they can influence their own futures. The more choices people can be given the better they will feel.

The key is, of course, early involvement and consultation so that the change becomes not your change but theirs. Consultation does not mean that everyone is consulted about everything, nor should it mean that managers pretend to consult having already decided the outcome. Rather, it means clearly delineating the 'givens' (what is *not* up for grabs in any change situation), but being prepared for people to exercise choice within these constraints.

Giving people control over change

A well-known company relocated its UK head office. This involved a massive programme of change over a period of almost two years and affected some 2,000 people. The change itself was a *fait accompli* and not up for negotiation. However, the company went to enormous lengths to involve and to give choice. For example, people were bussed over to the new site, they were given architect's presentations, teams were involved in selecting where their offices should be located, office layout, furniture, lighting and canteen facilities. The enormous amount of choice given in how the change was planned is believed to be a major factor in its smooth and effective implementation. Within two days of the new office opening it was 'business as usual'.

Of course, in this case it helped that the head office environment to which the company was relocating was a 'showcase', demonstrably better than before, characterized by its potted plants, vast palms and atriums. In a way it's a pity that the sensitivity employed in making the change didn't continue beyond turning the architect's drawings into reality. As it is, the walls in the office have been designed to prevent the attachment of any pictures or personal memorabilia, people have apparently become so desperate to make an impact on their 'designer' environment that they have envisaged covering the walls in velcro and flinging themselves against them!

However, the story of how this relocation was handled still contrasts very favourably with another corporate relocation. In this case, a large number of people were to be relocated from offices in Bracknell to Reading town centre. The personnel manager in Bracknell warned the director who was orchestrating the move that there was considerable resistance. 'I can't imagine why they're making such a fuss,' the director concerned said as he climbed into his chauffeur-driven car. 'After all, it's only 18 miles.' He had not even bothered to think about the implications for the people concerned. In fact, some of the issues causing the resistance were quite substantial and included:

- The building in Bracknell had excellent sports facilities; Reading had none.

- Bracknell had green spaces, fresh air and car parking, Reading had directors' car parking and legionnaire's disease.

- Some one-parent families' lunchtime shopping and home routines were disrupted.

- Transport to and from work was disrupted.

Does it take so much imagination to think these factors through in advance?

4.4.2 Why are you doing it?

It's clear that moving forward and making changes is much easier if you have some kind of better future to move towards. If the future looks as exciting as Scunthorpe on a rainy day, then why change? Senior managers frequently make the mistake of assuming that the reasons for change which are obvious at their rarefied level are equally apparent to everyone else and have transferred themselves into the organizational brain by some miraculous process of osmosis! Often the need for change is not clear at all, and people are not even sure what problem the change is supposed to address.

The clue for managing change is to give very visible leadership from the top, demonstrating the direction of change and the commitment of the top group. The top team should be first over the cliff and they should go on passionately selling their belief in a better future. It is vision which provides the powerhouse for change. In addition, the more people that can be involved in the external business realities of customer and competitors, the more they will 'smell the smoke and feel the fire'. Rather than telling people why the change, it's a question of involving people in discovering the need for change themselves.

4.4.3 Uncertainty and ambiguity

Change by definition means moving from the devil you know to the devil you don't. One can never entirely predict how the change will work out. Most of us dislike ambiguity and find excessive uncertainty extremely difficult to handle. Organizations are designed to create structures around people which make them feel safe. How, then, to persuade people to take unpleasant-looking risks? The antidote to uncertainty is to overdose on communications, to share information widely. This is a central tenet of managing change successfully, which we will explore in a later chapter. Information counts in building commitment to change.

Another implication lies in the type of people we recruit. If the rate of change is accelerating, then perhaps we need to recruit different kinds of people, people who have a high tolerance for uncertainty, mavericks, rebels. As it is, we tend to recruit 'clones', people in our own image. It is fascinating that at one stage in its recent history, Marks & Spencer apparently found the need to advertise for 'rebels' – their culture had been too successful previously in sifting out these troublemakers!

4.4.4   Springing surprises

The first and most natural reaction to the new and unexpected is resistance. Yet managers frequently make the mistake of springing change on an unsuspecting (or more likely partially suspicious) workforce. The approach is too often that of change by hand-grenade. Managers leap out of the cupboard with a grin on their face yelling: 'Surprise, surprise: we're going to reorganize/close down/make you redundant.' They wait until all the decisions have been made and then announce them. It's almost as though managerial machismo depends on the element of surprise and the extent to which the change has been decided down to the smallest detail before it is announced – tablets of stone descending on the uninitiated. Most people treated this way would ask: 'Why couldn't they trust me enough to give me a hint?' 'Why didn't they allow me time to get used to the idea?' Time and timing of change are crucial. It's amazing how the sheer passing of time removes objections. However, the reality is that people aren't given advanced warning and rarely given the space to accommodate themselves to change.

4.4.5   Loss of face

As all cultures, in both West and East demonstrate, people go to extraordinary lengths to avoid loss of face. If accepting a change means admitting that the way we did things in the past was wrong, people are guaranteed to view the change as a personal criticism and to resist.

Yet how frequently this happens. There is no more fatal kiss of death to a programme of change than for the change manager to attack directly the actions of his or her predecessor. This is the way to make enemies for life. New organization changes implicitly carry the message that the old ways were wrong. This automatically puts up the backs of those who grew under the old system and must now either look stupid or defend their past decisions. As those who prospered under the old system have frequently risen to positions of power, this can be a dangerous strategy!

Don't give people a chance to build a shrine to the past. Put the change in perspective. People did what was apparently the right thing to do at the time, but now the requirements have changed. Greiner shows the way with his concept that as organizations grow, what worked in the past won't in the future. There should be a 'no blame' clause, an 'amnesty' period between the old and the new ways. People can then see themselves not as incompetents but as strong and flexible in adapting to a different phase of business growth, which is after all the reality.

4.4.6 Can I cope?

Resistance stems from fear of the unknown and with good reason. Even with changes which we ourselves have welcomed or even initiated, the new situation will put us at risk. Nobody wants to be vulnerable and exposed. No one wants to appear inadequate or stupid, yet there will be concerns about future competencies as yet untested, about fear of failing and threats to self-esteem. Few of us feel we want to have to start all over again in order to feel competent – look, for example, at managerial resistance to using computer technology. There is always a learning curve in developing the new competencies necessary for the change and people need a great deal of help and support in the meantime. Part of this involves creating an atmosphere of trust, part is providing education and training in new skills, but an awful lot is just what the psychologist Carl Rogers calls 'unconditional positive regard', positive reinforcement which tells the team and the individual that they are OK, highly rated and can successfully make the change.

4.4.7 More work

Maintaining the status quo can seem exhausting enough, but change involves more effort, more energy, more time. This is ample reason to resist! Inevitably, things will get worse before they get better as people struggle to master the change. People begin to perceive themselves as stressed out. Their 'bucket' was full to the brim just coping with the previous workload; now additional responsibilities are being added. There will be considerable discomfort and stress, not so much for those who initiate the change as for those charged with making it work. Extra effort is required to reprogramme familiar routines or to absorb a stranger into a group. The additional workload which a change always causes means that a manager will need to be sensitive and react accordingly, for example, by being careful not to change everything at the same time, but to keep some familiar routines. Also by rewarding and recognizing the extra effort

involved, allowing people to convert themselves into believers in
change, finding some role models and rewarding those who practise
the new behaviours, not necessarily financially but through small,
immediate rewards like a 'thank you', a bunch of flowers, a special
trip, a dinner. As the 'one minute manager' would emphasize –
catch people doing something right and reward them little and
often.

EXERCISE 4

ASSESSING YOUR CHANGE PROBLEMS

Please use this worksheet to anticipate some of the major sources of
resistance you are likely to meet in engineering a specific change you
have in mind. What action can you take to convert the perception of
negatives into positives?

Change problems	Action options
1. Loss of control	
2. Why change?	
3. Too much uncertainty	
4. Surprise, surprise	
5. Loss of face	
6. Can I cope?	
7. Extra work	

4.5 Summary

The more you and your team understand the nature of the change
process, the easier it will be to reassure and prepare people for the
kind of problems and negative feelings they are likely to experience.
Understanding the process is the starting point for developing
sensitivity to change issues. There is no significant difference
between organizational change and personal change, the lessons are
the same. If you have to start from a central assumption, then it is
probably best to assume that change hurts as this will encourage

you to put in place the support mechanisms which will help individuals and teams to move through its predictable phases. Because the change process is predictable, it can, like any other management process, be managed. Understanding that most people perceive change as involving more negatives than positives will help you anticipate sources of resistance and use the seven pointers to change the perception of change and convert negatives into positives.

5

Building a culture for change

5.1 No quick fix

The essence of sustainable change is to understand the 'culture' of the organization you are trying to change. If proposed changes go against the grain of history and traditions, they will be very difficult to embed in the organization. Culture is created by messages which leaders, whether by accident or design, send out about what they really believe is important. One study of how leaders of organizations develop and transmit corporate cultures or climates identified several 'reinforcing mechanisms' (Schein, 1985). The full range of these primary and secondary reinforcing mechanisms is quoted by Simon Majaro in Figure 5.1.

The inner circle of the model represents primary reinforcement mechanisms, for example, the critical areas of how you reward people and who gets promotion. Leaders' reactions to critical events and crises are a very good test of how important the change is. If, in hard times, leaders say, 'Forget all that stuff, get your head down and get the sales out, that's all that's really important', then the change will not be sustainable. With the recession of the late 1980s early 1990s, many organizations have been encountering just this dilemma. The outer ring represents secondary reinforcement mechanisms such as organization structure and systems, but also the layout of buildings, what the company says about itself in its creeds and charters and who are the 'heroes'. If, for example, the people who are talked about and who get on in the organization are the bright boffin types in the backroom, then the organization can

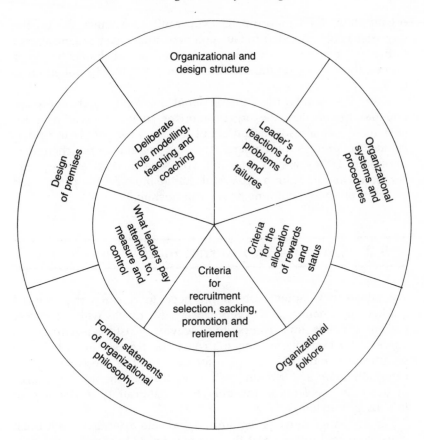

Source: Simon Majaro (1992)

Figure 5.1 How leaders transmit and entrench corporate culture

talk about 'customer orientation' as much as it likes, but it won't get the behaviours.

Well understood, these primary and secondary reinforcement mechanisms become the levers for change, the keys which can open up the willingness for change. This chapter will, in particular, draw out the learnings from the ICL experience to help you see how you can create a supportive culture for change.

Willingness for change cannot be created overnight. It takes many positive experiences of change before people learn not to be frightened, to take risks, to let go of the past and to trust that change will take them somewhere better. If people have previously had negative experiences of how change has been handled in the organization, then unfortunately you can't do a 'quick fix' on the day after you've decided to launch a new strategic or organizational initiative. Creating a culture for change means that change has to be part of 'the way we do things around here', it cannot be bolted on as an extra.

Before it's even worth thinking about developing a change plan, one has to sensitize the organization or create the readiness for change. We've already talked about the need for people to understand the process of change, and the reasons why change is necessary if they are to 'buy in'. To use a medical analogy, the surgeon who hopes for a successful change must get the patient in a healthy condition before he or she can operate.

5.2   Creating an internal market for change

We talked in Chapter 1 about the need to research the external market for change and keep closely in touch with changing customer needs and competitive activity. Customer satisfaction surveys, for example, or ongoing consumer panels can all help the organization anticipate and plan for new realities. Researching the external market and working with your team in the joint diagnosis of business problems is the only true justification and source of legitimacy for change.

Just as change must be legitimized and sold externally, so it must equally be sold internally if the organization is to mobilize commitment to change and achieve 'buy in'. It is very useful to think of the organization as an internal market for change initiatives, where opinions must be tested, attitude surveys used to benchmark internal perceptions and potential sources of resistance identified. We are frequently too arrogant with our external customers and we do exactly the same thing internally, telling the 'customer' that what we're 'selling' him is what he wants and that he'd better like it!

5.3   Investing in education

We started to introduce the ICL story in Chapter 4 as an example of the problems experienced in the very early 1980s, and the enormous levels of fear and resistance to change. We talked about the extent of the pain in the organization at that time. There's a lot more to tell in this chapter about the scale of ICL's investment in education and about its very conscious efforts to create a supportive culture for change. The story of ICL's transformation in the 1980s provides a very useful case-study for understanding change because of:

1. The dynamism of the environment and the rate of change which the whole of the computer industry has been experiencing in the last decade.

2. The power of the 'business case' for change in ICL. Without drastic change in the mid-1980s ICL, the only remaining computer mainframe manufacturer in the United Kingdom, would most certainly have gone out of business; it very nearly did in the recession of the 1980s. ICL was inward-looking, hierarchical and technology-led. It needed to be solutions-oriented, market-focused and responsive to specific industry sectors.

3. The fact that despite the obvious external and strategic reasons for change the organization proved so hard to move.

4. The honesty of the top team then and now in admitting the frustrations of leading change and their total commitment to getting good at 'doing' change as the essence of their competitive edge.

5. How they found mechanisms to 'engage' more than 20,000 people.

6. The sheer scale of the changes which affected every part of the organization – strategic, structural, systems, educational, cultural, attitudinal.

7. The effort which has gone into fine-tuning the infrastructure so that every aspect of the organization reinforces and sustains change.

Best of all, whatever ICL has done seems to have worked (or at least so far!). By the late 1980s ICL was consistently turning in returns on capital employed in excess of 50 per cent. Surviving its disastrous marriage with STC (Standard Telephones & Cables) and the happier alliance with Fujitsu, ICL will in the mid-1990s be going on to float itself as an independent business. The early story we will tell here about how ICL pulled itself up by the bootstraps is only the start. What is perhaps even more interesting is the ongoing story of how, under the chairman, Peter Bonfield, the corporation has capitalized on its early successes, sustained change and moved forward confidently into the very different environment of the 1990s.

In trying to make change happen in the 1980s the chief executive Robb Wilmot had somehow to get his people as familiar with the reasons for change as he was. He put 2,200 of his managers through a core programme, known variously as 'mind expansion' and 'the sheep dip'. It started top-down and ran for three years. The programme lasted 5½–6 days. The objective was to get managers to realize that things had to change. The event is now regarded as a watershed, a large part of the explanation of ICL's Lazarus-like rise from its bed of troubles. People came away saying 'I understand the problem', and the programme created a common language for ICL.

When a large, laconic American called Asa Lanum took over the Applied Systems division of ICL in 1984, the need for change had been recognized, but people's previous experience of change, the annual 'October revolution', had not been happy and the prevailing attitude was one of cynicism. A number of 'change workshops' had been planned to teach managers how to 'do' change to their staff. This was felt by the consultants concerned to be at the leading edge of training technology! Imagine their surprise when they were summoned to a Heathrow hotel to hear Asa say that change workshops were a great idea, but that every single person in the division of 500 people should go through them. He stated: 'Change can be exciting when it is carried out by us, but it may be disturbing when it is done to us.' Initially, resistance to the workshops was high – 'Why doesn't he just tell us what he wants doing?' But Asa stuck to his guns – the result was an excitement about change and a number of very interesting, self-generated projects.

The present chairman of ICL, Peter Bonfield, puts a lot of the credit for success on this huge investment in training. In 1990 alone ICL invested £20 million in training. Even larger-scale investments would be found in the case of Ericsson in Sweden or BP, who have both used education as the prime lever for creating willingness for change.

5.4 Total immersion in the business

Willingness for change comes from the feeling that there is no other option. Put a frog in a pan of water and gently boil it and the frog, failing to notice any difference in temperature, will apparently sit still until it is boiled alive. Many people in organizations are the same – they fail to perceive the phenomenon of global warming, that the temperature is rising and that evasive action is urgently needed.

This is why most of the famous examples of organization change are precipitated by crisis (BA with deregulation, Lloyds of London with the extraordinary losses of the late 1980s). The trouble is that while the top guys may long have recognized the crisis, when they yell 'over the top' they can turn round to find that there is no one following. How to make crisis real to everyone is the trick, to help all employees to be so closely in touch with the marketplace, customers and competitors that they diagnose the need for change for themselves.

Part of the answer lies in education, in giving people the experience of 'scanning their environment' and identifying pressures for change; part lies in formal communication from the top of what is happening in the business. But the real answer lies in persuading people at all levels to regard themselves as entrepreneurs in mini-businesses, closely in touch with their customers, responsive, interested and motivated by feeling they literally or emotionally have a 'share' in the business. There is nothing that focuses the head office manager's or administrators' mind quicker than putting them in front of things called customers and pound notes. Senior managers in BP Sweden, for example, are frequently seen manning the petrol pumps as part of their continuous immersion in the real world.

5.5 Shared vision

Later on we will talk about the vital importance of visionary leadership in creating the 'promised land', for it is only the thought of a better, different or more successful future which keeps us struggling with the problems of change. It's not enough that the vision should exist in the mind of the CEO, for as a recent *Fortune* article states:

> Yes a CEO must promulgate a vision, but the most brilliant vision this side of Paraguay won't budge the culture unless it's backed by action . . . CEO's encase their mission statements in plexiglass,

hand them out and people laugh. You have to change the way the person who assembles the machine or designs the product acts.

To be a real motivator for change, the vision must be owned by everyone. The ideal is summed up by the apocryphal story of the chairman being taken up to his penthouse suite by the liftman. As he chats about the company's plans to diversify into new businesses the liftman suddenly presses the emergency 'halt' button. 'Mr chairman', he says, 'with respect you cannot do this. It is inconsistent with our vision.'

Such is the power of organizations like The Body Shop, Sony or McKinsey. They have a clear vision and they spend enormous amounts of time and effort communicating it both within and outside the company. They get people excited about the destination which the company is aiming for, everyone knows where the bus is heading and everyone wants to be on board.

5.6   Spelling out the changing requirement

There is some interesting evidence that companies are focusing a lot of attention on task alignment, engineering gradual change by restructuring employees' roles, responsibilities and relationships. Here, for example, are the 'behavioural guidelines' which were written by Glaxo Pharmaceuticals UK as an outline for developing in the 1990s:

- **Responsiveness:** the capacity of the company to deal effectively with a marketplace in transition with flexibility and a sense of urgency.

- **Role clarity:** clear definition of job parameters so that each individual's contribution to outputs and objectives are understood and overlapping responsibilities are minimized.

- **Strategic and tactical balance:** employees to commit appropriate time to both long-term thinking and short-term implementation.

- **Cross-communication:** free communication across traditional boundaries.

- **Accountability:** the clear definition of responsibilities so that individuals understand both their contribution to achieving business goals and the scope of their decision-making.

Glaxo have gone further and have translated these roles and responsibilities into managerial guidelines, values and behaviours (see Chapter 7). These are the kinds of initiative which start to spell out the day-to-day working practices and behaviours which constitute long-term change.

5.7   Joint diagnosis of business problems

Parents spend a lot of time trying to teach their children not to make the same mistakes they themselves made. However, it rarely works. In life we have to make our own decisions and mistakes to acquire any real grasp of what's at stake. The same is true in organizations. We need to let individuals and teams reinvent the wheel. By helping people develop a shared diagnosis of what is wrong in an organization and what can and must be improved, a general manager mobilizes the commitment for change. It's not that anything new is learnt in a joint diagnosis. But those involved come to see clearly the organizational roots of a unit's ability to compete, and even more important they come to share a common understanding of the problems and potential solutions. When a specific proposal for change, such as a restructuring, comes along, you're halfway there because the climate for change is right.

5.8   Reinforcing a 'people matter' style

Young children can be very brave about exploring their world as long as their mother is nearby – a very tangible source of security. When she leaves they are likely to feel unsafe and to stop taking any risks. It's the same in organizations.

People who take the risks of change are those who feel confident about their self-esteem and security, whose personal and team identity is somehow protected. Hewlett Packard is a company famed for having developed just such a 'people matter' style, based around setting achievable targets, rewarding success, creating opportunities for celebration – generally making people feel good about themselves and the company.

5.9   How ICL created a culture for change

In December 1982 ICL had made its successful and much needed
rights issue of over £100 million. The financial crisis which two years
before had pushed ICL to the brink of bankruptcy was finally over.
Dr Robb Wilmot, who had been brought in from Texas Instruments
19 months earlier in a last-ditch attempt to rescue ICL, had cut staff
to 22,000 and imposed tough new management and budgetary
controls. However, he was already deeply frustrated at the slow
pace of change. As reported at the time in an influential series of
articles by Chris Lorenz in the *Financial Times*, he was 'leaping along
at 100 miles an hour but the rest of the organization was clanking
along at 50'. He could see what he wanted to achieve but he
couldn't pull the levers. As he himself said: 'I got frustrated. I
hadn't got an organization to understand or do it.' He went on to
say: 'No company without the commitment to build this sort of
organizational capability will be around in European electronics by
the end of the decade.'

ICL is still very much around and in its link with Fujitsu has gone
from strength to strength. The joint efforts of Robb Wilmot and his
successor Peter Bonfield to build the capability for change have
become a fine example of overcoming organizational resistance.
Peter Bonfield has described the challenge as making people 'more
receptive and less cynical to innovation and change'. This has meant
increasing the ability to respond quickly to change but also to initiate
it. In 1986 he said: 'We're now prepared to change the strategy
quickly and the organization with it. Two years ago organizational
changes stunned the company and people went into a state of
paralysis. Now we're doing them all the time.'

So how has ICL achieved such a huge attitude shift? It's
interesting to look at what has been done under the headings of
unfreeze, change, refreeze.

5.9.1   Unfreeze

Unfreezing creates the motivation and readiness to change and is
critical to the success of any change programme. ICL at the time
would probably have said that it was this part of the change process
that they understood least well. 'Unfreezing' involves encouraging
dissatisfaction with the current way of doing things and creating
both an external and an internal market for change. Unfreezing is

vital because without it people can so easily regress and revert to their old ways. What ICL did do through the internal management training programmes described earlier was to help managers understand the nature of the change process, emphasizing the negative emotional reactions to change which they could expect. This helped to 'unfreeze' the management population by moving it from 'unconscious incompetence' to 'conscious incompetence' and eventually 'conscious competence'. 'Unconscious competence' probably takes a lot longer to achieve, just like driving a car. Achieving a recognition of 'conscious incompetence' is vital in establishing that there is in fact a problem in managing people through change.

5.9.2 Change

The prime vehicle for achieving strategic and organizational change for ICL in the 1980s was education. In total a three-pronged attack was used to shift attitudes dramatically:

1. A management programme (approximately 1,000 managers) moving through a Stage 1–Stage 4 series of modules, Stages 3 and 4 specifically addressing the management of organization change in a complex company and developing strategic capability for change.

2. A marketing training programme (approximately 3,000 marketeers and senior business managers) to effect a change from a technology- to a market-led orientation, supported by immersion in a customer-oriented mission and the move to a business centre style of organization structure. This programme developed a common language for change in ICL and helped to break down communication barriers between functions.

3. Quality improvement programme (all 20,000+ staff).

The level of investment in creating receptiveness for change was phenomenal. Saturation training focused the mind to dramatic effect. 'Continuous investment in management development is just as essential as on-going spending on technology,' says Robb Wilmot. For example, between mid-1983 and the start of 1985 ICL spent more than £3 million – a chunky 10 per cent of its then less than spectacular profits. Peter Bonfield is convinced that the pay-off from education has been enormous: 'It has played a vital part in changing attitudes and cultures.'

5.9.3   Refreeze

Refreezing means reinforcing the message of change so that resistance does not re-emerge to drag people back to the old ways. The vocabulary used in ICL to describe 'refreezing' was 'institutionalizing', typically in connection with processes and procedures but also in terms of identifying and publicizing successful change experiences. As Don Beattie, group personnel director, says: 'It's tight supporting processes which maintain the new behaviours and stop people reverting back to their old ways.'

ICL was ruthlessly systematic in reviewing its management processes. It adopted a four-stage approach to 'investment in people':

1. Review all job descriptions.
2. Review technical career paths.
3. Review appraisal systems.
4. Review pay structures.

And a very thorough job they did of it too. First, the overall ethics or values of the business were codified in 'The ICL Way', a statement of the seven basic commitments expected of every man and woman in the company and the ten obligations of the ICL manager. First and foremost of the seven commitments was 'Commitment to change', the words used are interesting:

> Success in our company now depends on each individual's willingness to accept change as something valuable, something to be welcomed, something to be responded to with energy and resourcefulness. Our business is change. Our opportunities arise from change. To succeed in today's markets we have to predict, manage and exploit change in technology, in software, in manufacturing techniques, in marketing and selling. Therefore ICL managers and employees have to be able to respond fast and effectively to all the risks and challenges of change and to adopt new attitudes and practices willingly and creatively whenever the situation demands.

Second, an unusual process of organization and management review (OMR) was instituted. Quarterly management reviews were linked to the strategic planning process and ensured that changes anticipated in the business-cycle were supported by organization capability. The business review stressed new strategic thrusts, key operating plan elements and organization culture change objectives. In assessing whether they had the organization capability to make these changes happen managers looked at organization structure, management staffing and management processes. This sophisticated OMR process built a bridge between strategic change and organization change, which greatly helped to turn intentions into reality.

Third, ICL's 'Manager's Guide for Appraisals' ensured that all managers were appraised against the seven basic commitments and ten obligations of management. Guidance to managers included appraising individuals against their willingness to change.

ICL manager's guide for appraisals

The focus is on changes which have occurred in the person's:

1. **Job:** additional work, different work or products
2. **Interfaces:** new customers/ICL colleagues/locations
3. **Output:** additional or different end-results/objectives

The individual showed that he/she could move quickly through the normal reactions to a change (i.e. shock, emotion, rigid acceptance) into effective, even enthusiastic use of that change.

1. Put forward proposals relating to any of the change areas listed above which would improve productivity
2. Express dissatisfaction with the status quo.

Finally, ICL instituted an 'excellence award' scheme which provided recognition of outstanding performance against 'The ICL Way' commitments and created 'heroes' who were visibly practising and being rewarded for practising the new behaviours. This process started to develop career paths which encouraged the emergence of effective change leaders and provided a way of encouraging others to climb aboard the change train.

5.10 The lessons for sustaining change

The ICL experience shows all too clearly that corporate transformation is not for the faint-hearted and that it will involve realigning

> 'Structure, processes and culture are like a three-legged stool.
> If you don't pay attention to all the legs, it falls over.'
>
> David Pascall, Chief Financial Officer, BP

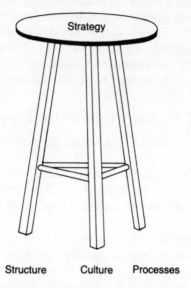

Structure   Culture   Processes

Figure 5.2   Reinforcing change

almost every aspect of the organizations systems, processes and structures, not just on a one-off but on a continuous basis. Our overall change model, 'How to create, manage and sustain business change' (Figure I.1, p. xii), emphasizes that building a culture for change means not only the initial stages of 'sensitizing' and creating an internal market for change but the final reinforcements of change which create the mechanisms which will sustain and embed the change over the long term.

These lessons are exemplified not only by the huge changes within ICL, but within many other corporations who are transforming themselves: for example, BP and Ericsson, the telecommunications giant. If, as Sir Robert Horton former chairman of BP has said, you are trying to create an organization that 'works, thinks and feels entirely differently', then there will be a knock-on effect in every part of the organization. David Pascall of BP has summed this up beautifully in his model for reinforcing change (Figure 5.2).

Ericsson is another most impressive example of creating a culture for sustained change. The corporation employs more than 70,000 people in 80 countries in telecommunications and electronic defence systems. The company was set up some 120 years ago, has sales of over 40 billion krone and a formidable reputation for engineering and research expertise. During the 1980s they bought into computers, failed and sold out. The pressure for profit was on. They made substantial changes and then they reinforced them by a re-examination of almost all their personnel, planning and reward systems. For example they have:

- Created a Management Education Institute for the top 1,500 managers across the world as 'management training may be the most important way of building integration'.
- Reinforced the HR (Human Resource) function: 'We think it is more and more important.'
- Instituted counselling: 'We saw how difficult it is to understand new values when people are wedded to the old technical values.'
- Identified a profile of skills, assessment, education and training run by the chief executive and a steering committee.
- Instituted a 'totally new' reward system for the top 1 per cent of Ericsson, worldwide.

EXERCISE 5

CHECKING YOUR CULTURE

Exercise 5 gives you some headings against which to do a spot check of your organization to assess whether the climate is likely to encourage willingness for change. It will help you identify danger signals and action points.

Spot check: dangers signals

Does your culture (the way you do things around here) exhibit any of the following characteristics?	Yes	No
Previous negative experience of change High levels of insecurity Too much security/inertia Low risk-taking Mistakes remembered/punished Strong demarcation across functions Closed, not open communications Entirely output-oriented Setting people up for failure, non-achievable targets		

Creating a culture for change

Do any of the following need attention in order to sensitize people for change?	OK	Needs attention
1. Is there an internal market for change? – dissatisfaction encouraged – regular internal attitude/opinion surveys – joint diagnosis of business problems		
2. Are you investing enough in education to change managerial mind-sets for the future?		
3. How closely in touch is everyone with the business environment? – everyone has some customer contact – presentations on competitive data, environmental changes – local autonomy encouraged		
4. Is there a shared vision of where the business is going?		
5. Do you have a 'people matter' culture?		
6. Are successful change experiences identified and publicized?		
7. Do career paths encourage the development of change leaders? Are 'heroes' rewarded?		
8. How is willingness for change institutionalized in formal systems of business planning, recruitment, appraisal and career development?		

5.11 Summary

Unfortunately, positive attitudes towards change cannot be created overnight. 'The way we do things around here' takes a great deal of time and effort to develop if it is to reinforce willingness for change. Building a culture for change means selling change into an internal market, as well as immersing people in the external market and environmental realities. The best way of sensitizing people for change is saturation levels of training and education which start to spell out the different attitudes and behaviours which the future will demand. Because change involves a new situation of high uncertainty, there is every likelihood of people feeling vulnerable to risk, mistake and punishment. The more people's self-confidence can be reinforced, the more willing they will be to take the risk of change. ICL provide a marvellous case-study of how over at least five years it has worked hard to create a positive culture, moving attitudes of 'change hurts' to attitudes which say 'our business is change'. What does a quick 'health check' of your own corporate culture reveal?

6

Anticipating and managing resistance

6.1   Resistance and the status quo

In the last chapter we looked at a case example of building a culture for change from the early stages of 'unfreezing' attachment to the past through to 'refreezing', consciously reviewing and revamping systems and structures to reinforce the change. In this chapter we look in more depth at the early stages of creating an internal market for change: the start of mobilizing commitment. If you want sustainable changes, then there are great risks in ignoring the resistance which will be an intrinsic part of the process. This is because the 'unfreezing' process won't fully have taken place and therefore people are likely to revert to their old behaviours the minute the market gets tough, or when you or the pressures go away.

Ironically, resistance can actually be the powerhouse which provides the energy for change. Selling change to the internal market means not just reinforcing the benefits but really listening to sources of resistance. This chapter provides a sort of plumber's 'toolkit' of techniques, which can help you harness the power of resistance.

Resistance to new initiatives is quite normal. If you already have what you need, why change? As CJ might have said in *The Rise and Fall of Reginald Perrin*, I didn't get where I am today by changing! As we've seen, change always involves heightened levels of uncertainty. Arthur Schlesinger Junior once said: 'Few are prepared to abandon cherished assumptions for admitted risks.' And as every politician knows, when you reform anything you increase the opposition of those who wish to stay with the previous regime. Machiavelli recognized this when he wrote: 'The reformer has enemies in all those who profit by the old order and only lukewarm defenders in all those who would profit by the new.' Even more striking are the comments made by Mikhail Gorbachev in his book *Perestroika*:

> Repeated attempts to reform the upper management levels without support from below were unsuccessful because of the stubborn resistance of the management apparatus which did not want to part with its numerous rights and prerogatives.

The paradox is that those with the highest investment in the status quo, who have been most successful in the past and around longest, will probably be the most active in resisting change. Yet they will contain among their ranks the loyal, the influential, the experienced and the senior. We are all products of our past. The challenge of organization change is to change ways of thinking which have been moulded over many years and have since become inappropriate. In the 1990s this is particularly a problem with the middle management layer of large organizations, who have become the 'cement'. Yet if change is to achieve critical mass, somehow the cement must move.

The great trap for both managers and politicians is to back off from, underestimate or fight resistance. Mr Gorbachev was guilty of all three – puzzlingly negligent in handling resistance he tried to isolate reactionary comrades, then ally with them and finally outface them. Since his own disastrous early attempts at change when he stirred up a veritable hornets' nest, Boris Yeltsin was thereafter much more active than his predecessor in courting the resisters, going out of his way to meet officers and men, being careful not to ruffle the feathers of vested interests. Even so, resistance eventually caught up with him!

Resistance to change, like a sales objection, can, if properly handled, increase the commitment to buy in to the change. A 'Zen', or 'judo' approach to going with resistance can be a more effective technique than confrontation or denial. But first of all we need to remind ourselves of where resistance comes from and how it can be anticipated and actively engaged.

6.2 Organizational and individual inertia

As we saw in Chapter 4, it is intrinsic to understanding the change process to realize that most of us spend most of our time resisting change. Our resistance stems from a horrid suspicion that we are about to encounter some or all of the following:

Resistance stems from:

Fear of the unknown

Lack of information

Threats to status

Threats to established skills

Fear of failure

Reluctance to let go

Lack of perceived benefits

Threats to powerbase

Low-trust organizational climate

History of previous custom

Fear of looking stupid

Feeling vulnerable and exposed

Threat to self-esteem

Loss of control of one's own destiny

Loss of team relationships

High anxiety

Stress

If individuals behave like this, then it's hardly surprising that whole organizations full of people take a lot of moving. How does one engage the hearts and minds of every employee of the 120,000-strong BP, or every postman in the mighty Post Office or every linesman in British Rail? These are leviathan organizations where the challenge of change can seem a bit like sticking a pin in an elephant. Again, in kick-starting the engine of change in the then USSR, Gorbachev brilliantly summed up the challenge in a way equally appropriate to any manager:

Waiting for instructions from above, relying on top level decisions has not yet been done away with. The point is that people grew unaccustomed to thinking and acting in a responsible and independent way. Here lies another big problem . . .

The supertanker organizations and ideologies of the 1980s cannot turn quickly enough to accommodate the rate of change of the 1990s. Organizations of vast size and hierarchy are now trying desperately to become a more flexible and adaptable kind of organism or a federation of smaller businesses. IBM's attempts to change its structure drastically to respond to a new market reality is a case in point.

Inertia is the thick treacle which convinces us of our powerlessness. While finding the need to seek permission is sometimes comforting, most people also greatly resent dependence on others. Here is Rosabeth Moss Kanter's famous spoof recipe for creating inertia:

Rules for Stifling Innovation

1. Regard any new idea from below with suspicion because it's new, and it's from below.

2. Insist that people who need your approval to act, first go through several other levels of management to get their signature.

3. Ask departments or individuals to challenge and criticize each other's proposals. (That saves you the job of deciding; you just pick the survivor.)

4. Express your criticisms freely and withhold your praise (that keeps people on their toes). Let them know they can be fired at any time.

5. Treat identification of problems as signs of failure, to discourage people from letting you know when something in their area isn't working.

6. Control everything carefully. Make sure people count anything that can be counted, frequently.

7. Make decisions to reorganize or change policies in secret, and spring them on people unexpectedly. (This also keeps people on their toes.)

8. Make sure that requests for information are fully justified, and make sure that it is not given out to managers freely. (You don't want data to fall into the wrong hands.)

9. Assign to lower-level managers, in the name of delegation and participation, responsibility for figuring out how to cut back,

lay off, move people around, or otherwise implement threatening decisions you have made, and get them to do it quickly.

10. Above all, never forget that you, the higher-ups, already know everything important about business.

Organization inertia might seem to be a depressing fact of life, but it also represents opportunity. Amazing things happen when people take responsibility for themselves.

Steve Shirley: converting the inert into the empowered

Steve Shirley is the millionaire founder of FI Group, the information technology management company. In the early 1960s, software was not the sophisticated tool it is today. When Steve decided to charge for software advice, 'everyone said it was impossible to have an organization selling something that was normally provided free'. Today FI has sales of £25 million. By the late 1970s Steve Shirley faced another dilemma, 'one of the hardest things for a founder entrepreneur is to know when and how to let go . . .' After hiring a chief executive in 1987, Shirley took a back seat and began to think seriously about handing over the reins completely. 'We had developed a professional albeit part-time workforce, a professional management, a corporate structure and identity – which coupled with my beliefs concerning freedom and getting the best out of people left me little choice. The next step, obvious to me, was to offer employee ownership.' In a share sale to employees in 1991, she reduced her holding to 35 per cent and handed over voting control.

Steve Shirley has reversed every one of Rosabeth Moss Kanter's 'rules for stifling innovation'. She has liberated her people to get on with running the business, which so far they are doing successfully; she has liberated herself to move into a statesman-type role, such as becoming the 'Master of the Worshipful Company of Information Technologists', the 100th City guild in London. Organizational inertia has become organization empowerment.

6.3 Identifying resistant forces

It becomes crucial to identify and anticipate sources of resistance to change at the beginning of the change process. If, for example, resistance is particularly overwhelming, then it may be much better to abandon that particular change and try something else. Take Mrs Thatcher and the poll tax, for example, where all the writing was on the wall long before the change put people's resistance sky high and it ultimately failed in spectacular fashion. Here are a selection of directors' comments emerging from a workshop where they were asked to identify resistance factors to a business and organization change in their UK subsidiary of a major chemicals group. The rueful realism of their observations is striking and sad. The words are their own, although for obvious reasons the company is disguised.

Company X: directors' comments on resistant forces

Failure of communication

- 'The reasons for change have been communicated very badly.'

- 'If you wanted one phrase, it's "failure of communication". That's the basis of the whole problem.'

- 'Nothing is going to work unless we motivate the commitment and energy of our people.'

- 'What you really want would be to get the whole company together on site somewhere, saying this is what's happening, these are the reasons for it.'

- Q 'Is there any particular date anyone has in mind for the next round of significant communication?'
  A. 'Yes, last April, but we didn't make it.'

Resistant groups

- Groups of middle managers are much more likely to be resistant.

- Middle management people who have not been involved in changes because the project group activity has generally been confined to directors or heads of departments. A lot of middle managers have been there for life.

- Unions will defend the old ways of doing things.

- There are pockets of people at shopfloor level more difficult to persuade because they are people who have been there for ever . . . it's simply a question of inertia and may be more than resistance.

Defensiveness and fear

- They have a large number of people with very long service. There is not much turnover. There is a degree of defensiveness and fear.
- They feel threatened by the changes, some of the service departments will need to change their structures and reduce their staffing levels.

Unrest/uncertainty

- They don't know what the structure or products are going to be, so there is more unrest in this area.

More work

- What they are saying is: 'Oh God, they are going to occupy space, they are not having any of my space, how is it going to affect my job', and 'Oh God, I've got to work for them too and I'm already overloaded.'

Past reputation

- We have the reputation of a hire and fire company, people's feelings of security are probably not overdeveloped because they've seen or heard what happened in the past.

Lack of commitment

- I'm not convinced that everyone is prepared to push for this.

This example provides some crucial learning points in terms of why people resist, who will tend to resist and how management action – or lack of it – makes things ten times worse. The 'why resist' is related to people's level of investment in the old way of doing things and their reluctance to move away from the known and the familiar. The question of people's level of security and insecurity is an interesting one. If people are too insecure because of the company's reputation as a hire and fire business, they will be very aware of the reaction to past mistakes and will quite sensibly be reluctant to put their necks on the line. Equally, if people have been there for ever, with long service records and little fresh blood from outside, they become too secure and still won't change! Managing change means managing the tension between security to the point of inertia and insecurity to the point of psychological risk. This means that for people to change they must believe that the organization is in trouble and that their personal survival depends on doing something differently. But they must also feel that they are in a safe learning environment, not about to be beaten by the old carrot and stick.

The question which the example poses as to who resists suggests that there will be pockets of resistance around the organization, very probably where the old ideologies are still strong but increasingly being challenged, such as at shopfloor level, within unions or at middle management level. Middle managers, increasingly at risk with the slashing of workforces and the creation of flatter organizations, can, as we've seen, be particularly resistant. It's interesting that in Sweden, Ericsson encountered such a big problem in overcoming middle manager resistance to change that they instituted special seminars, groups of 10–12 middle managers, just to discuss their situation – 'they need to talk'. Interestingly, they concluded: 'It is very easy to get them back on track.' Wherever possible they made attempts to 'put them on important project teams'. Perhaps the learning point is that where there is a particularly resistant group, who perceive themselves as standing to lose a lot through the change, action is a better policy than hoping the problem will go away.

Finally, the example shows that failure of communication lies at the heart of most botched programmes of organization change. If managers were allowed one wish, it should be that they keep talking about change as openly as possible and as early as possible. (More about this in a later chapter.)

Where change evolves on a gradual basis, involving the key players over a period of time, resistance can be minimized or eliminated. However, when, as is more usual, change is communicated as a *fait accompli*, then resistance levels will shoot up – out of shock if nothing else. There is always an 'X' factor in change: the cost of change both in productivity and in human terms. Unless the resisting forces are exceeded by the factors going for the change, then the change will not happen, there is no momentum to make it do so. This is summed up well by the change equation shown in Figure 6.1. This equation states that unless dissatisfaction with the current state of affairs plus the desirability of the changed future, plus the do-ability of the change exceed the cost of changing, then there will be no movement. One can see this formula working in everyday life; indeed, it could almost be used to predict whether a particular change will overcome natural resistance. Think of moving house. You may be entranced by a new house and pretty dis-

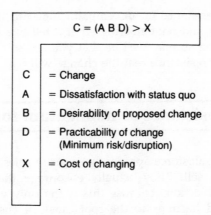

Figure 6.1 Managing resistance: the change equation

satisfied with your current accommodation, but just think of the cost of changing, the disruption, packing and moving – and then think again . . .

Projected split of gas/oil companies in the United States into two separate businesses

It is hardly surprising that resistance to the proposed change is so high given that few people can see any advantages in the proposed scheme, nor anything wrong with the current way of organizing the business. (extract from consultant's report)

Identifying sources of resistance means anticipating the impact of a change on both people and the business. To get an idea of the size of the change and probable levels of resistance try 'scoping' the change by asking yourself questions such as:

How many of m_· colleagues will be affected?

Will team identity be broken up?

How much retraining will be necessary?

What about 'at-risk' individuals such as one-parent families?

Will relocation be needed?

Will the change affect career opportunities?

Will there be an impact on domestic/shopping/travel arrangements?

Is a change of boss involved?

The Essence of Change

Identifying resistance means empathizing with the pieces on the
wargame board and remembering what it felt like down there. The
cost of not doing so may well be that you are so out of touch with
the scale of the resistance that the change will fail.

6.4 Resistance as momentum for change

A professional salesforce apparently regard a sales 'objection' as an
opportunity to sell. They actually encourage their customers to
express their objections because this is the only way they can get
beyond the red herrings to the root cause of customer doubt. A
customer who hasn't got any objections is not engaging – he is
either disinterested, asleep or dead. Perhaps we should apply the
same approach in managing change. It's all right for people to resist
change – we expect it, anticipate, even encourage it. By expressing
their own resistance people can convert themselves into believers in
change.

The practical advice for any manager would be 'go with the flow',
rather than counter-punching with the arguments why that particular change is such a good idea. This seems counter-intuitive, like
leaning out from the slope when ski-ing, but it can work. A bit less
'macho' and a bit more 'Zen'. A judo approach, backing off from
the attack, can be very productive in changing the balance between
the change 'initiator' and the change 'resister'. Good sailors know
that when two sailors are both leaning out in an equal and opposite
attempt to stabilize the boat, it will fail to move. One of them must
do something apparently irrational, by transferring his weight into
the boat. Balance between the resisters and the forces for change
produces equilibrium; and equilibrium means no change.

6.5 Some techniques for managing resistance

We touch here on three of the techniques available for managing
resistance:

1. Counselling.
2. Force-field analysis.
3. Commitment charting.

6.5.1 Counselling

It's amazing the extent to which simply letting people talk through their problems and doubts can help them come to terms with change. The Samaritans, of course, have practised this for years and 'the talking treatment' is a familiar part of psychotherapy. Within business there is a range of methods you can use, from informal sessions in the pub to one-to-one counselling meetings, from management by walkabout to formal communication sessions with the whole team. If you take the latter course you will need, in addition to any formal input, to structure time for small 'break-out' sessions as few individuals will admit their anxieties in front of a large number of their colleagues.

6.5.2 Force-field analysis

This technique was devised many years ago by Kurt Lewin through his researches in the United States. It provides a practical technique for assessing in any change situation the likely balance between the driving forces and the resisting forces. The first step is to identify the forces going for the change and those likely to go against the change. This can be done by the 'change agent' or, even more usefully, by involving the team who will be going through the change. Figure 6.2 is an example of a team of middle managers from the Innovex group assessing a major company reorganization.

The conclusion which the Innovex team drew out of their force-field analysis was that there was a strong and convincing business case for making the proposed organization change, in terms of both increased client focus and internal integration. However, they recognized that powerful sources of resistance could only be minimized if they took action to research the internal market and establish very careful communication channels.

Innovex's business depends on its skills in developing and selling a 'process' for organizations to manage clinical trials research in getting new drugs into manufacture as quickly and painlessly as possible. They found that they had to do exactly the same internally, in building their capability to manage change. They needed to create a shared change process for thinking through specific changes, a simple 1–10 checklist or discipline, which the entire management team would follow from inception to implementation. This they have started to do and they believe that the more they use it, the more they add layers of competitive advantage to their internal capability.

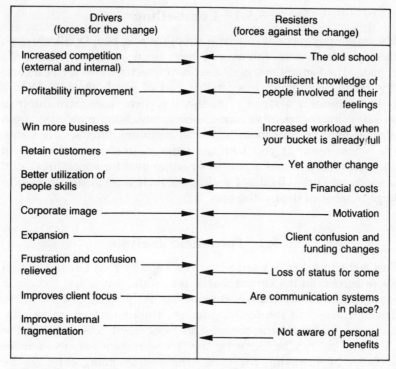

Figure 6.2 Innovex group: force-field analysis of company transformation

Innovex's change process

Here is one of the early change processes they came up with to handle the change outlined in their force field analysis. It shows they are heading along the right lines:

1(a).   External market research and communicate the 'why' to divisional heads and senior managers.

1(b).   Research internal market, two-way diagnosis of problems, identify sources of resistance.

2.   From 1(a), feedback results in 'family' groups, give them some time to think and then take group feedback, give key individuals time to think and talk individually.

3.   From 2, match current with future core competencies, give training, establish current workload, stresses.

4. Ensure understanding through formal and informal communication channels, use anonymous response questionnaires, ensure there are no casualties, everyone knows everything.
5. Check again.
6. Schedule the change realistically over three months in small chunks, check and validate as you go.
7. Validation through internal surveys and surveys of client satisfaction, on-going training and development.

Going back to their force-field analysis it would be easy to assume that the best way of overcoming resistance would be to sell hard on the benefits of change. In fact, research shows that there may be much more mileage in choosing to spend time and effort minimizing the resisters. Again, using the sales analogy, many professional sales personnel emphasize the importance of accepting and handling objections to the sale rather than just pushing ahead on all the reasons why the customer should buy.

Innovex learnt that by manipulating the 'resisters' they actually provided themselves with levers to swing the change in their favour. For example, carrying out internal anonymous audits helped with the second source of resistance by giving them more knowledge of how people were feeling in the organization whilst individual counselling reduced the resistance to an increasing workload. It's fascinating that Sir Winston Churchill well understood and worked a similar process during the Second World War when he had informants all over England to report to him on morale levels in the factories. Confronting the bad news – that strike rates were higher than in peacetime, that the East End was near to outright rebellion – enabled him to seize these levers and through an intensive internal PR campaign waged energetically by himself and the present Queen Mother to swing the resistance in his favour. Sometimes there will be many positive drivers for change and just one key resister. The action that managers take to manipulate this key resister can spell the difference between a change that can be implemented and one that will fail.

Some teams of managers having carried out their force-field analysis find it useful to attach a numbered weighting to each factor so that a total score can be arrived at, and the balance of drivers against resisters more accurately assessed.

In applying the technique to a particular change you may find that the particular change you are proposing is unlikely to be viable. We're always told that the first rule of financial management is that accountants don't like nasty surprises! Anticipating levels of resistance in this way can help any manager contemplating a significant change from perpetrating and receiving a nasty surprise!

6.5.3   Commitment charting

In any change there will be winners and losers. Clearly, it is particularly important to target in advance the potential change losers so that they can be handled with sensitivity and their pain minimized. There is also the question of gaining critical mass for change. This is likely to be very difficult in the early days of the change when there will be few early innovators and an awful lot of people either sitting on the fence or running in the opposite direction. This is where the technique of commitment charting can be so useful (see Figure 6.3). Based on the work of Beckhard and Harris, this approach examines the motivation of the key players in the change on a scale from active antagonism to a positive intention to make the change happen.

The 'X's indicate where that person's commitment is at present, the 'O's indicate where their commitment needs to be to ensure that

Key players	Antagonistic	No commitment	Let it happen	Help it happen	Make it happen
1.			X ————————	——————	▶ O
2.			X ——— ▶ O		
3.			O ◀————————	—————— X	
4.			O ◀— X		
5.			(X O)		
6.			(X O)		
7.			(X O)		
8.			(X O)		
9.		X ————————	—————— ▶ O		
10.	X ————————	—————— ▶ O			

Source: Adapted from Beckhard and Harris (1987)

Figure 6.3 Sample commitment chart

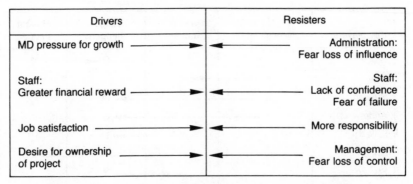

Figure 6.4 Growth through delegation: drivers and resisters

the change is successful. The arrows indicate the work that must be done to shift individual attitudes. Player No. 1, for example, can be placed in the 'let it happen' box, but his active desire to 'make it happen' will be needed. Player No. 10 is positively antagonistic to the change and while it is not essential that he himself drive the change, he must somehow be persuaded to go along with it passively. Interestingly, Player No. 3, who is currently very 'gung ho' about the change, must be pulled off and persuaded to let go and let it happen. By making it his change rather than the team's change he may be seriously jeopardizing success. Where the 'Xs' and 'Os' coincide in the same box XO, then, as in the case of players 5, 6, 7 and 8, we can breathe a deep sigh of relief and direct our attention elsewhere.

Elliot Brothers Audio Sounds Ltd

Bruce Elliot set up Elliot Brothers Audio Sounds Ltd in 1979. They are in a very interesting business sector – specialist engineers selling services to install radio stations and recording studios. By 1990 their turnover was £1.5 million and the business employed twenty-five people. Bruce was trying to move the business from Greiner's Phase 2 into Phase 3 'growth through delegation'. On the back of an envelope he sketched out his force-field analysis (Figure 6.4) and his commitment chart (Figure 6.5).

These analyses posed some interesting issues. Should Elliot back off from trying to drive the change through? Whose change was it anyway? How to increase the 'buy in' of two key members of the team, how to persuade Chris not to be too enthusiastic. In terms of

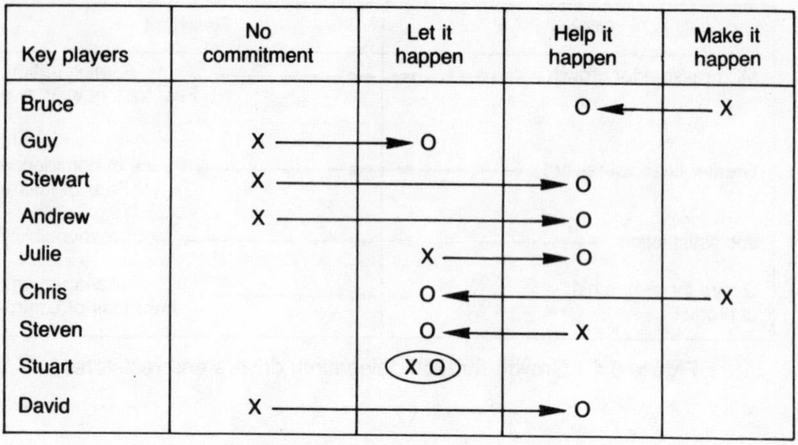

Key players	No commitment	Let it happen	Help it happen	Make it happen
Bruce			O ◄——— X	
Guy	X ———► O			
Stewart	X ——————————► O			
Andrew	X ——————————► O			
Julie		X ———► O		
Chris		O ◄——————————— X		
Steven		O ◄——— X		
Stuart		(X O)		
David	X ——————————► O			

Figure 6.5 Commitment chart

his 'force-field analysis', Bruce is never going to get his new plans to
take root until he tackles the empowerment dilemma of a Board who
fear that they will lose control of the business and a staff who
haven't got the confidence to take responsibility for themselves. His
critical actions need to be here.

EXERCISE 6

**PREPARING A FORCE-FIELD ANALYSIS AND COMMITMENT
CHART**

Exercise 6 provides you with blank pro formas for completing both a
'force-field analysis' and a 'commitment chart' for your business.

The process of force-field analysis

1. What is the problem/change issue?

2. Where are you now?

3. Where do you want to get to?

		Driving forces	Resisting forces
4.	What are the things going for the change?		
5.	What are the resisting forces?		
6.	What action can minimize resisting forces and maximize driving forces?		

Sample commitment chart

Key players	Active resistance	No commitment	Let it happen	Help it happen	Make it happen
1.					
2.					
3.					
4.					
5.					
6.					
7.					
8.					
9.					
10.					

X = Where that person's attitude is currently.
O = Where he/she needs to be for the change to happen.

6.6 Summary

Most people naturally resist change. By anticipating, identifying and even welcoming resistance, we give ourselves the chance to convert raw objections into the energy for change. Rather than counter-attacking with the arguments 'why this change will be good for you', we might do better to adopt a 'judo'-like stance of going with the flow, absorbing and reflecting. It's amazing how the process of merely allowing people to express their fears and resentments helps them convert themselves into believers. The technique of force-field analysis helps identify and weigh up sources of resistance against the arguments for making the change, allowing us the opportunity, either to rethink whether it is the right change in the first place or to take action to reduce the 'resisters' and/or accentuate the 'drivers'. Commitment charting helps identify whose change it is and the work which needs to be done in persuading key players and minimizing painful effects on any change losers.

7

Visionary leadership

It is the vision of a new future which provides the pull-through and momentum for change. Developing this vision with his team is perhaps the single most important job of a leader. It is visionary leadership which recognizes the early signs of commitment and by communicating and magnifying them throughout the organization creates a sustainable change.

This isn't just a 'loudspeaker' job from the chief executive, it involves giving people time and space so that they convert themselves into believers. After all, leadership means two things: first, providing vision and direction, knowing where you're going; second, persuading other people to go there! A recent *Harvard Business Review* article outlines 'six steps to effective change' and by doing so defines the role of the visionary leader (see Figure 7.1).

It is interesting that the language used to define the leader's role is 'develop', 'foster' and 'spread' rather than 'sit in your office and dream up a vision statement, which you then impose, top-down, on everyone else'. In this chapter we will look at a set of practical tools and techniques to help you create a genuinely shared vision, which will link your strategic intent with the power in the engine room of the organization. We will also look at how organizations such as Glaxo Pharmaceuticals have led change and some of the dilemmas their leaders have encountered. We will encourage you to look again at your own leadership style and how you 'role model' change.

1. Mobilize commitment to change through joint diagnosis of business problems.
2. Develop a shared vision of how to organize and manage for competitiveness.
3. Foster consensus for the new vision, competence to enact it and cohesion to move it along.
4. Spread revitalization to all departments without pushing it from the top.
5. Institutionalize the change through formal policies, systems and structures.
6. Monitor and adjust strategies in response to problems.

Source: 'Why change programmes do not produce change', *Harvard Business Review*, Nov./Dec. 1990

Figure 7.1 Six steps to effective change

7.1 The vision thing

The process of change begins with 'what-if-ing', hypothesizing and inventing new possibilities, from which one can look back at the past situation and as a result start to shift from the predictable past to a possible future. It is moving step by step towards a different and potentially more desirable future which enables us to take the pain and let go of the past. As the editor of *Fortune* magazine said: 'The new paragon of an executive is a person who can envision a future for his organization and then inspire his colleagues to join him in building that future.'

Getting people on board with change means giving them a destination they want to go to and then spending a lot of time painting a picture of what it will be like when they arrive. It is amazing the extent to which inaction can be the response in the face of a set of problems which are clearly recognized intellectually. Hearts and minds do not necessarily follow each other. In other words, managers and employees have to be won over emotionally as well as rationally. They have to commit themselves to a new vision and accept the personal costs of transforming that new vision into reality. The journey of change will only be undertaken if the cost of transition is made bearable by a compelling image of the promised land (see Figure 7.2).

'I have a dream,' said Martin Luther King, that is, 'vision': imaginative, emotional, passionate, inspirational or, as Mr Gor-

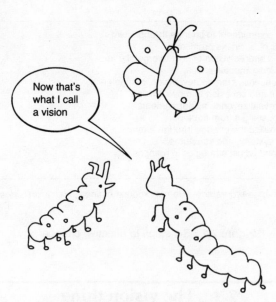

Source: *The Economist*, 9th November 1991

Figure 7.2   The vision thing

bachev said, waxing positively lyrical: 'So if you can see this lofty
goal, a shining temple on a green hill, then the heaviest of stones
are light, the most exhausting work a pleasure.'

The visionary, of course, can easily be accused of being crazy and
sometimes is, but it is the people with the attractive and compelling
dreams who create successful companies and motivate people
towards continuous change. Vision is all about why your company
does what it does, its underlying philosophy. It should be the
lodestar to everyone in the company. It is the power and passion of
the vision which will translate paper strategies into life. Vision is
everything that a mission statement is not, it has no finish line, no
time limits, no quantifiable measures. It lives and grows as a
description of where the company wants to be. It is a visual picture
painted in words – think of Italy's Benetton or Switzerland's Swatch,
or America's Disney or Japan's Sony, all companies where a
visionary fervour has outlived early entrepreneurial origins.

Visions and visionaries

Here are a few of the leaders who demonstrate just how powerful
vision can be:

- Sophie Mirman (ex-Sock Shop) talking about her new enterprise in King's Road selling up-market children's wear and called 'Trotters':

  'We shall keep this company small and keep it private. The service has got to be 100 per cent. It will be impeccable. We want it to be a small enjoyable business. We want everyone to have fun with it.'

- Sheila Pickles who transformed 'Penhaligons', an ailing perfumery business, into an international empire worth $128 million, a company founded on the nostalgic vision of one woman (as was Laura Ashley).

- Anita Roddick, chairman and founder of Body Shop says:

  'A vision is something you see and others don't. Some people would say that's a pocket definition of lunacy. But it also defines entrepreneurial spirit. To succeed in something you have to believe in something with such a passion that it becomes a reality . . . we communicate with passion and passion persuades. You can be proud to work for the Body Shop, and boy does that have an effect on morale and motivation. Since 1984 when we went to the Stock Market our obsessive vision has been to act as a force for social change.'

- Between 1965–1982 Komatsu, a Japanese manufacturer of earth-moving equipment, lived a vision described as 'Encircle Caterpillar' (then the world's largest manufacturer). In 1965 this vision looked ridiculous, Komatsu was a small, weak player with no presence outside Japan. But it was crucial to have this focus. It wasn't possible to plan the vision in detail, but over many years, layer upon layer of competitive advantage was carefully laid down. They succeeded.

7.2   Building a shared vision

Some years ago the chairman of a huge British multinational was reputed to have sat down in the privacy of his office to write the vision and shared values for over 100,000 staff! As visions should and usually do have a longer shelf-life than chairmen, it's generally a good idea for the manager of a changing business to involve his whole team in creating, owning, sharing and living the vision. One

managing director, outlining his vision on a development programme at Cranfield, commented: 'We've had it for some years but
we haven't told anyone about it.' What a missed opportunity!

Here is how two other famous businesses went about building
commitment to a shared vision.

Sir John Egan of Jaguar and Steve Jobs of Next

Jaguar, now part of the Ford group, has had a long and chequered
history. The era of 1928–72 was typified by immense loyalty to
owner/founder Sir William Lyons, passionate belief in a distinctive
product characterized by 'grace', 'pace', space', and a vision of
engineering excellence. The BL era of 1972–80 saw commitment to a
vision of a luxury racing car wither. In 1980, when Sir John Egan
took over at Jaguar Cars as chairman and chief executive, he took
time to communicate the new vision through a 'hearts and minds'
programme for all Jaguar employees and their families. Here is just a
flavour of the sheer scale of the sporting and social programme
during 1982 and 1983 alone:

- Jaguar fun night (280 runners plus spectators).
- Bonfire night celebrations (17,000 attended).
- Open day attended by 36,000 people.
- *History of Jaguar Cars*, a free hardback for employees.
- Inter-departmental sporting competitions (1,700 people).

Steve Jobs has proved to be an extraordinarily visionary leader in
the computer world. After leaving Apple, he started a new business
called 'Next Computers'. He took the entire management team away
for a retreat. During this retreat he argued, shared and fine-tuned so
that his vision demonstrably became the team's vision. The only
technology they used was a flip-chart board. After Jobs' short
presentation on his dream, its importance to him and why he
thought it exciting, the flip-chart board was rapidly taken over by
other members of the team to demonstrate how they intended to
make the vision a reality.

Building a shared vision doesn't mean going through a mechanical process. There is no simple formula for coming up with instant
vision, and there is a lot of unhelpful mythology around, for
example:

- Vision is created only by the person at the top.

- The vision will be a detailed blueprint, spelling out a grand plan where outcomes and paths will be fully explained and an arrival point achieved.
- A vision is an elegant statement under nice neat headings.
- Visions are short-lived and won't outlast the next crisis.

The reality is very different. Organizations are now far too complex for any one person at the top to be solely responsible for formulating the vision. This expectation that someone at the top will tell the rest of us how to change is part of the problem. We need to allow for different groups to take leadership in sponsoring different issues and for many interlocking 'visions' from country managers, product managers, functional managers. Visions like dreams can't be too specific, for the vision charts an unknown and unknowable world – 'there be monsters here'. Strategic change is an iterative process involving many small steps which can't all be seen at the beginning of the change. Sometimes the best one can do is keep one's eyes fixed to the mountain top, like Fujiyama in a haze – somewhere over there. A vision means real passion and real communication; it cannot be bought by the yard in the management bargain basement. If the vision of the mountain top disappears every time the direction of the path or the weather or a new summit comes in sight, then it is no vision.

Building a vision with your team probably means thinking through with them some of the following questions, but none of them can have pre-programmed answers:

- Why are you bothering to run this business at all (instead of, say, selling off the assets and shutting up shop)?
- What is your personal crusade/your own passionately held belief?
- What can your company offer that your competitors can't?
- What unique contribution can your company make?
- What epitaph would you like on the gravestone of your company?
- What would you like people to be saying about your business, i.e. the press, the City?
- What would you want people to miss if your company was liquidated?
- What does your business do that makes any difference in the world?

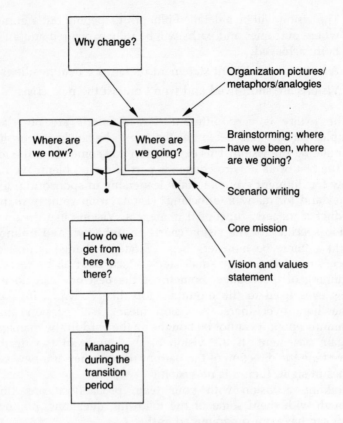

Source: Adapted from Beckhard and Harris (1987)

Figure 7.3 Building a shared vision

- What is it that others call 'impossible' which you can make possible?

Because 'envisioning' is such a very creative process, many of the techniques of creative thinking, of opening up, challenging and exploring are very appropriate; some of them are considered below under the framework provided by Figure 7.3.

Figure 7.3 also helps to tie us back to our original model of the elements of the change process. The question 'why change?' was addressed in Chapter 1, and organization diagnosis or 'where are we now?' in Chapter 2. Clearly, before we can get on to the issue of how we manage the transition process and put together a change plan, we must identify where it is that we want to go in the first place! As the former manager of the New York Yankees once said: 'If you don't know where you're going, you might end up somewhere else.' Building on the Beckhard and Harris model, we offer a 'menu' of simple tools, which you can use in gradually working with your team over time to create a vision.

Above all, developing your business vision as the driver for change isn't a job you can do in isolation or overnight. It takes time, lots of team meetings and much questioning and deliberation. It should be a gradual uncovering rather than a 'flavour of the month' initiative. Here are some of the approaches you can use.

7.2.1 Organization pictures, metaphors, analogies

Getting people to sit down in a group and draw a team picture of how they visualize the business now and into the future can provide a revealing insight into the 'visionary' process, for a picture paints a thousand words. Some of the pictures or images of the future we have seen recently include:

- A flock of geese on the wing, a 'V' of individuals who know the common goal, take turns leading and adjusting their structure to the task at hand. Geese fly in a wedge but land in waves.

- A circus ring: 'Ladies and gentlemen, the combined skills and synchronized talents, all under one big top.'

- A formation of Red Arrows flying with safety and precision, a quality organization, achieved through the involvement of the whole workforce.

- A TQM hospital, compassionate and caring aiming at prevention rather than cure, open communications and no 'us' and 'them' type elitism.

As part of a famous questionnaire on career and life planning, individuals used to be asked to describe a perfect day in their life, say, five years from now. The way people visualized the balance between home, work, leisure, creativity painted a revealing picture of the kind of future they were aiming at. And so it is with organizations, although such an exercise is clearly only a way of opening up the thought process and generating new ways of looking at things. Other useful techniques include using comparisons and metaphors to try to pin down the essence of the future the management team is trying to build. Most of us are familiar with the game of imagining what the business would be if it were an animal (a growling tiger or an affectionate dog) or if it were a newspaper (the *Financial Times* or the *Sun*). Many of the creative thinking techniques pioneered by Edward de Bono are immensely useful in visioning, in providing a paradigm shift to get us out of the normal thought patterns and give us a new perspective from which to examine a familiar situation. In 1968 de Bono invented the phrase I 'po', derived from words like 'hy(po)thesis', 'sup(op)se', '(po)ssible' to allow us to set up what he called 'provocations' – new perspectives on old situations. We might then, for example, compare a management development change with a gardener's challenge in planting a seed, or hypothesize ('po') issues to do with a reorganization by forcing a comparison from any random word such as 'cigarette' or 'cow'.

7.2.2 Brainstorming: where have we been, where are we now, where are we going?

Brainstorming with your team a list of words and phrases which describe the characteristics of the company historically now and into the future can give a powerful insight into the kind of company you 'want to be' (apologies to the Prudential's advertising campaign). Figure 7.4 gives an example from some work done some years ago by the management team of Innovex.

Doing some navel-gazing in this fashion has helped Innovex to translate the strong vision of the owner/founder, Barrie Haigh, into a vision of the kind of future the entire management team wants to build. Innovex has worked hard to retain some aspects of the past, for example, being an open, non-political organization. Other

Historical	Current	Future
Cosy comfy country cottage Slightly chaotic but a very happy family Small team playing bar billiards Top line driven Passionate attempt to avoid politics Exciting, a buzz	We're in transition losing some of our specialness We tolerate failure (which is good) Still a bit disjointed Reorganization and management changes	International Experienced elder statesman Polished and professional Excellent with customers Attract and keep terrific people Spin-off separate units

Figure 7.4 Innovex: brainstorm of historical, current and future desired characteristics (carried out in 1988)

aspects – for example, becoming international and building management maturity – are being constantly developed.

7.2.3 Scenario writing

We touched on the technique of scenario planning and scenario day dreaming as a way of scanning the business environment in Chapter 1. Scenario writing was developed as an approach to long-term planning and technological forecasting. Herman Kahn, one of the pioneers in the field, explains its usefulness as a visionary technique in change management. Scenario writing:

- Reduces 'carry-over' thinking from the past.
- Plunges one into the unfamiliar and rapidly changing world of the present and future.
- Tackles details and dynamics which might easily be neglected by a more abstract consideration.

Scenario writing helps the management team to become more receptive to change and to creative thinking and provides a deliberate and systematic technique for doing so. Ultimately, the most valuable aspect of scenario writing is not its accuracy but the fact that managers have shared a process which opens their minds to new possibilities and opportunities. The process challenges perspectives and provides an alternative worldview. It is well described by Simon Majaro in his 'Pocket MBA' series on *Creativity and Innovation*. The technique hinges on members of the group scanning their business environment (technology, suppliers, legislative trends, economic trends, etc.) and anticipating the impact of the most significant areas of change on their area of specialization over the next 5–10 years. This is usually done individually with short papers and presentations to the group and then collectively by the group. It is a kind of 'what if' process, developing alternative scenarios of what life might be like in the future.

7.2.4 Core mission

Vision isn't mission, but businesses also need a challenging, short-term goal to help form part of the clear image with which company employees can identify. Much has been written about mission statements, which should, of course, have a measurable finish line (you should know when you've got there) and be achievable – just. Mission provides focus and clarity and may be worth revisiting in the search for a powerful future vision. Here are some examples of admirable punch and clarity:

- **McKinsey Consulting Group:** 'To help our clients make positive, lasting and substantial improvements in their performance and to build a great firm that is able to attract, develop, excite and retain exceptional people.'
- **Honda faced with Yamaha:** 'We will crush, squash, slaughter Yamaha.'
- **Pepsi Cola:** 'To beat Coke!'
- **The new CEO of a British engineering company** (asked by his bank manager about his mission): 'My mission is to get you buggers off my back.'

7.2.5   Vision and value statements

Another approach for trying to change the mind-sets of managers towards the future is to involve them in articulating a corporate credo or philosophy, as Robb Wilmot did in 1983 in ICL, summed up by 'The ICL Way'. It still sums up the ICL philosophy. Similarly, Ericsson, the mighty Swedish telecommunications giant, is as lively and enthusiastic as any small entrepreneurial business when it states its core values in the form of the three musketeers: 'Perseverance, Professionalism and Respect'. One of the most famous examples of creating and transmitting a vision of the business which people passionately believe in is Johnson & Johnson. Here is their corporate credo. It might appear to be just a lot of 'motherhood' statements but the difference is, if you talk to any J & J employee they mean them!

The J & J Credo

We believe our first responsibility is to the doctors, nurses and patients, to mothers and all others who use our products and services. In meeting their need everything we do must be of high quality. We must constantly strive to reduce our costs in order to maintain reasonable prices. Customers' orders must be serviced promptly and accurately. Our suppliers and distributors must have an opportunity to make a fair profit.

We are responsible to our employees, the men and women who work with us throughout the world. Everyone must be considered as an individual. We must respect their dignity and recognize their merit. They must have a sense of security in their jobs. Compensation must be fair and adequate, and working conditions clean, orderly and safe. Employees must feel free to make suggestions and complaints.

There must be equal opportunity for employment, development and advancement for those qualified. We must provide competent management, and their actions must be just and ethical.

We are responsible to the communities in which we live and work and to the world community as well. We must be good citizens – support good works and charities and bear our fair share of taxes. We must encourage civic improvements and better health and education. We must maintain in good order the property we are privileged to use, protecting the environment and natural resources.

Our final responsibility is to our shareholders. Business must make a sound profit. We must experiment with new ideas. Research must be carried on, innovative programmes must be developed and mistakes paid for. New equipment must be purchased, new facilities provided and new products launched. Reserves must be created to provide for adverse times.

When we operate according to these principles the stockholders should realise a fair return.

7.3   Leading change

Senior managers are often themselves products of the old system and may find it very difficult to initiate or lead a change which reverses their prior decisions and stances. The classic way of signalling change in an organization is to put someone new in at the top, but this person too will need personal courage for he or she will be embarking on a change process where it is not possible to predict the outcomes either for himself or herself or for the organization.

We have said that 'vision' cannot be the property of one person at the top of the company, but this in no way belittles the vital importance of visionary leadership in organizations which are changing. The more things are changing the more necessary it is to have someone at the top who sums up, models and articulates the vision for the future. Models of leadership are themselves changing and the perception of the leader as a person of huge charisma with an ego to match is breaking down. The *Financial Times* recently stated of a famous company chairman, 'he is not held back by a lack of self-esteem' and indeed when this particular individual met his demise it was partially because his top team had got fed up with tottering under the weight of his giant ego. Or as Attila tells us in *The Leadership Secrets of Attila the Hun* (Wess Roberts): 'seldom are self-centred, conceited and self-congratulatory chieftains great leaders but they are great admirers of themselves.'

As we saw in Chapter 3 with the 'strategist' questionnaire, the trouble with the hero is that he creates dependency in the organization and actually reinforces the status quo. The landscape of the modern organization is far too complicated for one person, who may walk on water a few times but is then in trouble. He or she is playing a losing game, as leadership expert Ronnie Heifetz indicates:

> Because the entrepreneur is inclined to accept responsibility and to see himself as hero or heroine, he's also inclined to say 'OK, I'll do it again for you. I'll pull the rabbit out of the hat like last time. In fact I pulled it out the last two times. And watch I'm going to do it this time too. The entrepreneur is energized by those expectations. And if he does save the day he's reinforced the expectation that he'll be able to do it again and again. But it's a losing game . . . because by now there's no one around who has any capabilities. Every time he pulls the rabbit out of the hat, he generates more dependency and weakens his constituency, his own company. That's the trap in becoming a hero. (From Face to Face interview, *INC*, October 1988)

The essence of visionary leadership lies in the activity of orchestrating the resources of others in solving problems – not in being the hero oneself. Unfortunately, many chief executives learn this lesson the hard way. They like to keep on being the hero. That's one reason why at a certain point even the most successful CEOs have to leave, because there is a dependency on them which they can't shift. They can't let go. Most senior managers will want to learn the transition from meddler to strategist to avoid becoming a constraint on the growth of their own organization. The essence of visionary leadership lies in two aspects: first, articulating the vision, and second, in mobilizing the energies of all people towards the vision.

The managers of Innovex have a clear expectation of their chairman, Barrie Haigh, whom they regard as a visionary leader: 'His role should be to lead ten paces ahead, like a magnet, dragging us after him and challenging our way of doing things.' This beautifully sums up the role of senior management in the change process, that of constantly alerting the management team to new challenges and threats, giving them alternative worldviews, and forcing managers to reconsider and rethink their basic approaches and favourite old recipes for success.

This role becomes particularly vital when proactive change is preferred to crisis change. At first crisis change appears easy. The crisis provides the legitimacy for changing systems, changing structures and hiring and firing people. Without the crisis, indeed possibly even with it, senior management may be very reluctant to go for strategic redirection if it means relinquishing power. So starting to 'do' change through changing the powerbase may appear efficient, but can also be very traumatic in terms of the human costs associated with change. It is preferable to spare the organization both the cost of waiting for an obvious crisis and the trauma of responding to it suddenly. Proactive change means gradual evolution, continuous change, and this starts with the mind-sets of key managers, using education rather than power structures to achieve change. This is where the visionary leader's role in constantly challenging the team to think the unthinkable is so vital.

Thinking the unthinkable: leading change in Glaxo Pharmaceuticals UK (GPUK Ltd)

Throughout the 1980s Glaxo, the British pharmaceutical giant, was spectacularly successful. Over the decade profits grew from £66 million in 1980 to £1.2 billion in 1991. £1,000 invested in Glaxo shares at the end of 1980 was worth £27,400 by the end of the decade (against £6,570 if the same sum had been invested in an average UK general unit trust). Glaxo manufactures the best selling drug in the world, Zantac, and in early 1993 actually topped the *Financial Times* 100 list as Britain's biggest company, with a stock market capitalization more than twice as large as ICI's. A success story by any standards.

But the 1990s are bringing a new set of imperatives. External pressures could well provide a series of bone-jarring knock-on effects as the NHS works its way through changes in purchasing power and new relationships with suppliers result in fragmented markets and cost-conscious health authorities. Glaxo must also come to terms with the Single European Market and the competitive activity of not just the giants but previously tiny 'blips' on the radar screen, such as the Swedish Astra, described by one Glaxo manager as 'a rowing boat with a huge bomb on board'.

Yet there is no obvious crisis in sight, as there was to galvanize British Airways after deregulation, or IBM in the early 1990s. So why change a winning formula? Glaxo can only guess at the next as yet unseen crisis. Yet as an organization it is trying to be visionary, shaping the future and fighting against complacency. Executive chairman of Glaxo Holdings, Sir Paul Girolami, is far from complacent in identifying the need for constant change:

I think we are entering a new phase of economic development. The model of great success in the past will not serve in the next twenty years. Models change, we mustn't assume that we can progress in future from the grasp we've had in the last twenty years. The whole nature of the industry is being transformed.

Sean Lance, former managing director of the UK subsidiary and now of the whole UK operation, was asked: 'When will all this change end?' He replied: 'It won't end, that's the point! Success only comes from adapting to the changing demands of the market-place and the external environment and you know these are always changing.' His concern has been that 'we were not organized in the best way to meet the challenge of the 1990s. Our attitude and behaviours were not likely to bring us as much success as in the 1980s.' Indeed, internal attitude surveys had uncovered significant levels of frustration, particularly at middle management level. Combined with the external pressures from the marketplace, these surveys provided part of the stimulus for change. A series of initiatives were introduced called 'Developing for the 90's', which aimed at challenging the mind-set of all managers and staff and opening up their thinking to environmental threats and opportunities.

The aim, as explained by Sean Lance, was 'to create an organization which is responsive to our customers and which will progress the flexibility and sense of urgency to deal with a marketplace in transition'. The framework for the future was spelt out through RATIO:

Role clarity

Acceptance of change

Teamwork

Innovation

Output orientation

A series of workshops were cascaded right through an organization of 2,000 people to help them:

- Understand the reasons why changes were needed.
- Understand what each individual needed to do to enable change to happen.
- Learn new behaviours to increase levels of co-operation and communication across the organization.
- Change attitudes towards change and working with each other.
- Start the process of reviewing working practices.

There were many taskforces and project teams using multidisciplinary groups across the organization to examine specific strategic questions and options. There were at least two central dilemmas:

1. Where can we find consistency of management values, if the average age is 32, most people have never worked anywhere else and there are few positive role models?
2. If middle managers are demotivated 'blockers', how can they be released and re-energized to make change happen?

Through a series of 'Leading Change' programmes the entire middle and senior management team of 250 people had devised and agreed 'GPUK: The Way We Work', a statement of the values and behaviours which they intend to commit themselves to for success through the 1990s. These behaviours build on the RATIO framework and are a superb example of real bottom-up change. They are summarized in Figure 7.5. All these processes and mechanisms are changing the mind-set of managers away from 'business as usual' towards a different kind of operation. They are raising the level of debate, challenging the very formulas that gave success in the past and signalling proactive change, constantly alert to other ways of looking at things. Considerable sums of money, time and effort have been ploughed into gradually shifting attitudes. Says Sean Lance: 'What is important is that I believe we are getting a significant and growing return from this investment in our key resource – people.'

We value

- Our contribution to the health and well-being of the nation.
- The relationship with our partners in the delivery of health care.
- Honesty in everything we do.
- The contribution of all individuals and their personal development.
- The learning which comes from listening.
- The effective use of all resources, particularly people's time, energy and commitment.
- The taking of responsibility for decisions and actions.
- Flexibility and responsiveness.
- Achievement.

Role clarity

In managing, we:

- Define and delegate responsibility.
- Support and advise.
- Remain accessible to staff.

In responding, we

- Are willing to seek and take on responsibility.
- Commit to agreed objectives.
- Keep managers informed.
- Ask for help when needed.

Acceptance of change

In managing, we:

- Take ownership for change and its communication.
- Seek the advice of relevant people.
- Recognize that change requires support.

In responding, we:

- Try to understand the need for change.
- Assist in the process.
- Openly discuss concerns and feelings.

Teamwork

In leading a team, we:

- Clarify objectives of teams.
- Share information.
- Respect and encourage all views.
- Champion the decisions of the team.

Figure 7.5 GPUK – The way we work

In teamworking, we:

- Encourage individual views and contributions.
- Communicate openly.
- Promote the outputs of the team.

Innovation

In managing, we:

- Recognize and reward innovation.
- Accept mistakes are a necessary part of taking risks.
- Listen to ideas and avoid critical responses.

In responding, we:

- Voice and develop ideas.
- Test ideas through experimentation.
- Learn from mistakes.

Output orientation

In managing, we:

- Agree stretching, realistic and relevant objectives.
- Hold reviews.
- Praise achievement and effort.
- Measure and reward outputs.

In responding, we:

- Participate in the development of objectives.
- Commit to deliver.

Figure 7.5–*contd.*

7.4 Living the vision

Actions always speak louder than words and when change is in the air people will watch the top management team closely for signals as to what they really believe. Middle managers won't use new management tools and processes until they see top management using them first. The power of the top team in role modelling the behaviour they seek is immense. As Deal and Kennedy (1988) say in their useful book *Corporate Cultures*: 'In order to build a strong culture, top management must be convinced that it can adhere faithfully and visibly to the values it intends to promote.'

Ericsson's vice president, in Stockholm, Per Olaf Akerberg, says:

'As soon as you have values on paper, you must demonstrate that behaviour. Everyone looks at top management, you mustn't do anything against the values.' Ericsson pondered the problem of how employees were to give feedback to bosses, subordinates or colleagues who were behaving in a manner which subverted their major changes. Among other things they invented the 'yellow card', a small plastic card with the mission and values printed on it, which is held up (or sometimes just 'accidentally' shuffled in the top pocket) to provide a clear non-verbal message. It is also fun!

BP Oil Europe take very seriously the importance of the top team 'living' the changes they are trying to make. Their aim is: 'We want to be always saying to ourselves that we are doing better than yesterday.' 'Walking the talk' includes senior managers being prepared to talk about their own problems and inappropriate behaviours and indicating that they welcome feedback. For example, the new general manager of BP Benelux, a Frenchman, has asked that people tell him when he is acting in his old, authoritarian way. There is inevitably a measure of discomfort and artificiality in the way senior managers are trying to signal change. For example, one European chief executive, when asked to bare his soul before a training group and explain what he personally was doing differently, replied that of course he would, but he felt like a small child being forced to sit on its pot when it didn't want to. BP Oil distributed a desktop stamp to all managers with the message: 'I'm trying to change, are you?' Some managers maintained that it should have read: 'You are trying to change, am I?'

Living the vision, being the role model for change, is actually exceptionally difficult. It puts senior managers at the fault line of the organization, trying to demonstrate the new vision while so many of the old behaviours linger on, and worse still are probably still rewarded!

The management and the executive committees of Glaxo Pharmaceuticals UK, of whom we spoke earlier, are, to their great credit, actively struggling with these dilemmas. They are perceived as extremely powerful role models and their behaviours are minutely observed and analyzed for the clues as to how the rest of the organization should behave in a time of transition. Some of their key decision dilemmas turn on:

- Who do we promote? The organization is full of very young, very bright, very ambitious people, who will do what they have to do to get on. Do we promote the politically astute, those who get their sales figures or those who are great managers?

- How do we deal with those who can't make the transition within a culture of openness and honesty?

- How do we maintain the externally and internally 'caring' aspects of our vision when times get hard?

- How do we create a learning organization and mechanism which will help us and others to get and give continuous, open feedback on behaviours?

- How do we turn empowerment into a reality when the organization is full of people who don't want to take anything that could be perceived as a career-limiting risk?

Fortunately, visionary leadership doesn't mean turning out 'clones' who all practise a particular management style. There is room for immense variety in the shape, size and methods of successful leaders. The important thing, as the Chinese philosopher Lao-Tzu said, is that 'When the best leader's work is done the people say – we did it ourselves.' How you create vision and inspire people to want to make it happen is up to you.

The following anecdotes – offered in a humorous vein – indicate some of the possibilities:

- An old Sandhurst joke goes 'Men will follow this officer anywhere – out of sheer curiosity.'

- Contrast Brezhnev and Gorbachev. No wonder little change happened under the repressive regime of Mr Brezhnev, who was clearly not overendowed with creative genius. On receiving Mrs Thatcher for a state visit he followed customary practice by reading his greeting from notes prepared by his staff. 'Dear Mrs Gandhi,' he commenced, to be interrupted by a horror-stricken official who pointed out: 'But this is Mrs Thatcher.' Mr Brezhnev is alleged to have replied: 'I know it's Mrs Thatcher but it is written here Mrs Gandhi'!

- After eight years as rector of the Royal College of Art, which he transformed, Jocelyn Stevens took over as chairman of English Heritage. 'Up on the top floor I found a notice announcing my appointment with giant red arrows pointing at it "The Piranha is coming!" Honestly, with a reputation like that, half the job is done before I get there.'

- 'Make mistakes faster then anyone else and never repeat any of them' (Michael Spindler, CEO of Apple).

7.5 The long goodbye

The Economist recently suggested establishing a kind of home for the great visionary leaders of the past, the Thatchers, the Gorbachevs who failed to survive the changes they themselves initiated. Corporate boardrooms are strewn with the debris of powerful chairmen who, having pointed the organizational bus in the right direction, are ejected before it arrives. Any change you unleash has a momentum all of its own. Because the reactions of people around you to the change will actually change the change, you cannot accurately predict the outcome. You may find that you are only the co-passenger, not the driver of the engine of change.

Hubris, as the Greeks remind us, was swiftly punished in the shape of Nemesis. It's always dangerous for the leader to believe his or her own publicity. As we've said previously, it is probably inevitable that even the most effective leaders will eventually outlive their usefulness to the organization – Steve Jobs at Apple, for example, Ken Olsen of DEC, Jan Carlsson of SAS. Contrast the boldness of Mr Gorbachev's early years with the slow agony of his political demise. It would be nice to think that the leader can pick his or her own time to go, just ahead of other people demanding it, and that when it happens he or she can feel that his or her life's work is complete.

EXERCISE 7

HOW VISIONARY ARE YOU?

A very useful guide to assessing your visionary leadership capability is the 'Visionary Leader' questionnaire by Dr Marshall Sashkin. It enables you to assess for yourself and, more important, get feedback from others on the characteristics which Dr Sashkin's research has shown to be associated with effect leadership.

Characteristics of visionary leaders

1. Focused leadership	Effective leaders focus on a few key issues.
2. Interpersonal skills	Communication skills in getting messages across to others.
3. Trustworthiness	The leader takes clear positions and avoids 'flip, flop' shifts.
4. Respect for self and others	The leader has genuine concern for others – what Carl Rogers calls 'unconditional positive regard'.

5.	Risk-taking	The leader is willing to take risks and doesn't spend his or her time in 'cover-your-ass'-type activities.
6.	Bottom-line leadership	Effective leaders have a sense of self-assurance and a belief that they can make a difference.
7.	Empowered leadership	Effective leaders don't want power for its own sake; they share power to give everyone influence. They 'empower' others.
8.	Long-term vision	Effective leaders are able to think over relatively long timespans of at least a few years.
9.	Organization leadership	Effective leaders help the organization to change.
10.	Cultural leadership	Effective leaders create, articulate and communicate shared visions and values.

Source: After Dr Marshall Sashkin. The Visionary Leader Questionnaire is available from MLR Ltd, PO Box 28, Carmarthen, SA31 1OT.

However, the only test that really matters when it comes to leading change is what you are doing within your own organization to encourage people both to anticipate a changing future and respond rapidly to its opportunities. This is where leading change becomes leading edge. The following can be no more than a guideline. You'll know whether you're both opportunistic and inspirational:

- Does your company really have a vision, a picture, a passion for the future (and we don't mean a piece of paper)?
- Are you the only one who knows about it, or is it truly a shared vision which the newest recruit and the most junior secretary are proud to talk about?
- Are you waiting for a crisis?
- How much are you doing to educate and alert your managers to potential opportunities and threats?
- How are you working with individuals and teams to challenge their ways of thinking and get them to unlearn what contributed to their past successes and discover new ways of managing?
- What do you personally stand for in the organization?
- How patient are you prepared to be in going for gradual sequential change rather than sudden reorganization?

7.6 Summary

It is a shared vision of the future which provides the pull-through for change and helps to overcome the costs of change intrinsic to the change equation. The more time we spend hypothesizing about the future, inventing 'what if' scenarios and visualizing new possibilities, the more we start to move away from the predictable past. Vision is a passionate, vivid picture of the future owned by the whole organization. Building a shared vision is time-consuming and can only be done by involving the whole team. The job of the strategist, the visionary leader is to draw out and communicate the vision, to ensure that his or her actions 'role model' this vision, and constantly to challenge the management team to think differently and reinvent the past. Are you a visionary leader? Heroes aren't wanted on the journey and should bail out now!

8

Destabilizing the status quo

8.1 Speeding up the unfreezing process

Many of our corporate examples show that even when a charismatic leader articulates a powerful vision for the future, change often doesn't happen. For an organization to change, it must first be destabilized, or 'unfrozen'. That is why shifting people out of their comfort zone is such an important part of the elements of a change process. It is interesting that one of the lessons which ICL have drawn out of their change experiences is that, if anything, they underestimated the amount of early attention which needs to go into 'unfreezing' the organization.

As change always involves increased anxiety, people are very reluctant to detach themselves from the safe and familiar past – unless, that is, there is an even greater anxiety that by *not* changing they will put themselves, their jobs or their colleagues at risk. To speed up the unfreezing process we need to induce this greater anxiety. This means creating a general perception that the current ways are no longer working. Change managers must make disconfirming data highly visible to everyone, and this means a great deal more than just announcing that the business is in trouble because profit levels are falling, marketplaces shifting or customers complaining. All too often employees simply do not understand or believe it when the management says 'We're in trouble', particularly if they have a long and comfortable history of success. It takes massive levels of communication and intense education to make this message sink in. People must also make a connection between the disconfirming data they are being given and their own actions, that if they don't learn something new they will fail.

But as usual there is an intrinsic change dilemma. We need to destabilize people in order to detach them from the old order, but equally we must then very rapidly create conditions of psychological safety, a learning environment, in which they can experiment with new ways and be supported, trained, encouraged and rewarded at each step in the process.

Centraal Beheer

Centraal Beheer is a general insurance company based in Apeldoorn in the Netherlands. It is the largest direct writer of insurance in the Netherlands with 2,300 employees and a great pride in its strong customer focus. As in many other insurance companies, the mid- to late 1980s saw hard times and their Group Insurance Division experienced severe economic difficulties. The Board gave senior managers twelve months to achieve demonstrable improvement. They created an anxiety greater than the risk of doing something different! They made a big investment in honest and open communications to staff of the business realities and the reasons for change. The anxiety spread. But staff were well supported through training and through the introduction of systems such as flexible terms of employment. They had a symbol for their struggle and their success: the beaver!

8.2   Immovable objects and irresistible forces: the dynamics of change

---

As the familiar song goes, when an immovable object meets an irresistible force 'something's got to give'. What 'gives' depends on the dynamics of change, as expressed in the change equation. If there is insufficient dissatisfaction with the status quo, then the immovable object won't budge and what goes under will be the change itself. Somehow we have to break the inertia of stagnation to a point where employees recognize that the present *modus operandi* cannot continue. Isaac Azimov, world maestro of science fiction describes in his famous *Foundation* saga, the fall of the Galactic empire through the irresistible force of inertia:

The psychohistoric trend of a planet full of people contains a huge inertia. To be changed it must be met with something possessing a similar inertia. Either as many people must be concerned, or if the number of people is relatively small, enormous time for change must be allowed.

We want actively to encourage people to criticize the current state of affairs and discover their own dissatisfaction with the status quo. It is the first step in the change dynamic. Ignore it at your peril for, without it and despite the most delectable vision in the world, movement will be paralyzed. Gorbachev made this point when he said: 'Of course perestroika [restructuring] has been largely stimulated by dissatisfaction with the way things have been going in our country in recent years.'

Pent-up anger and discontent are the motivators for change; no significant change is possible without them. Think of the break-up of an unhappy marriage – rarely will either partner make a move (despite the existence of apparently more desirable options) unless there have been long years of growing frustration and critical assessment of the problems. In business this means creating the leverage for change by stimulating criticism of the past and present, building active dissatisfaction and, if necessary, engineering a crisis. It also means keeping a constant weather eye on the change process to ensure that attitudes stay fluid enough to move forward rather than regressing to the old behaviours once the immediate threat has gone away.

8.3 Harbingers of doom

The pattern of organization change is almost always that shown in Figure 8.1, which ties in with the conclusions of Larry Greiner's research that the prerequisite for effective change is a combination of both external pressure, for example, from the marketplace or

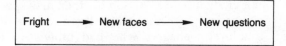

Figure 8.1 The pattern of organization change

shareholders, and internal pressure created, for example, by attitude surveys revealing widespread dissatisfaction or by the appointment of a new person at the top. It is the fright, combined with the new face(s) at the top, which permits unaskable questions to be asked.

Appealing to reason is not enough to uncover the need for change; it is therefore very useful to have visionary leaders who challenge the organization or prophets of doom who predict catastrophe unless ways are changed, like Hari Seldon, the 'raven' who, in Azimov's *Foundation & Empire*, predicts disaster, that Trantor will be ruined and that the decline and fall of the Galactic empire is inevitable. Organizations need some of these maverick characters who are clear-sighted enough to see that the emperor has no clothes and brave enough to publicize the fact. Leaders must develop ways of encouraging dissonant information and allowing the 'devil's advocate' view in decision-making. Alfred Sloan, President of General Motors in the 1920s, used to say that if all the Board was in agreement, then all he knew was that the decision had to be the wrong one!

Although new faces at the top are typical of the destabilization period of change, it is also possible that a kind of internal harbinger of doom can be built into the organization by developing the habits of continuous criticism and self-criticism as the antidote to complacency.

8.4   Surfacing dissatisfaction

All revolutions are seeded in active discontent. Equally, evolutionary change in organizations demands that we identify shortcomings and develop alternatives, that we are constantly looking for better ways of doing things.

A software house in Manchester

In the mid-1980s a Manchester software house ran a large workshop on 'managing change' for part of its business. The people who took part fell into two main camps. On one side there was a group of very bright young graduates and PhDs in the then new specialism of 'knowledge engineering'; on the other there was a group of middle-aged, mid-level managers who had grown up with the organization. The first group were change-oriented, had little investment in the past and were highly committed to finding better ways of doing things. They were enthusiastic in bringing into the open the problems and issues of the organization; there was enormous dissatisfaction with current processes and a great commitment to finding better solutions. In the case of the second group the reaction was overwhelmingly one of not wanting to air their dirty linen in public. It's easy to see which group was creating momentum for change and which group stifling progress. If people refuse to see that there is anything at all wrong with past or current practice, then they will be completely closed off from the possibilities of change and not even the shiniest of visions will get them moving.

As the amazing John Harvey Jones has frequently stated, the engine of change is dissatisfaction with the present. Glasnost opens up the organizational can of worms to the appraisal of all and thereby provides a powerful momentum for change. As Gorbachev once said, 'We need no dark corners where mould can reappear.' Gorbachev firmly believed that no radical change is possible without developing habits of criticism and self-criticism and without creating a forum for airing grievances. It is said that after the intiation in the USSR of daily television broadcasts, the political awareness of the people grew more in three weeks than it had in the previous fifty years – they got an insider's view of government. It unleashed a new rebelliousness and allowed the revolution from below, which spelt both the end of Gorbachev and the beginning of real change.

Anita Roddick explains how innovation in the Body Shop depends on breaking the rules, doing it differently. She says: 'We'll provide an arena for debate and discussion – a chance for people to make their voices heard. We will be a vehicle for challenge and change.' There are many mechanisms which you can use for taking the lid off the organization and encouraging managers and staff to peer in at the maggots. It is extraordinary how well people will respond to a change which deals with real problems which they recognize. Typically, a new CEO will commission an attitude survey, which is likely to reveal widespread dissatisfaction and therefore legitimize the chief executive's cries for change. Management consultants can be useful diagnosticians (particularly the small one-man bands), think-tanks, working parties, quality circles, brainstorm sessions are all good ways of trying to bring problems out into the open to acknowledge that the present is not perfect and that change is needed. The Rowland report on Lloyds of London, the pressure for an independent statutory agency to regulate the City in the wake of the Maxwell mess and the Blue Arrow trial, are all ways of trying to bring murky issues into the light of day.

8.5   Recognizing a common enemy

Part of the destabilization process lies in recognizing that there is a new threat to the organization which demands a new response. Generally, however, it is better if the enemy is without, not inside the organization. Because of the growing fragmentation of organizations as the old vertical structures break down it is often a case of the enemy within – marketing if you're sales, one division if you're another, head office if you're out in the regions. The enemy within is usually not a stimulus to productive change.

However, the joint recognition of an external threat has the marvellous effect of rallying the troops around a change and creating a sense of purpose and movement. There is no such thing as a 'Swiss', only a Bernese or a Zuricher – until, that is, an Austrian appears on the scene! This doesn't necessarily mean waiting for a crisis. It can become a continuous positioning of the organization in awareness of its competition, like Pepsi Cola's stance against Coca Cola – an ongoing motivation for gradual change.

It's sadly true that one of the traditional problems in changing huge organizations such as the Post Office or British Rail or the large insurance companies has been that employees have a strong sense of inviolability and don't recognize external threats to their survival. At one stage, when the Post Office was very actively trying to change from the top, the reality with some postal workers at the grassroots was that they only felt they were a part of a team when they defined their own section manager as the enemy! There's no time to fight external battles when your energies are used up in internal skirmishes. It would be interesting to assess whether this attitude has now shifted in the mighty Prudential, for example, in the light of the changing financial market, their disastrous venture into estate agencies and the pressure on margins. Perhaps even thick-skinned elephants are beginning to feel the pin-pricks of external threat and enemy action.

8.6   Engineering a crisis

Breaking the rules is an essential part of innovation. This means going in the opposite direction to everyone else, taking one's thinking outside the 'box' so that from a new position one finds new ways of looking at things. Entrepreneurs often attribute their success to the fact that they look around at what everyone else is doing and then do the opposite. They become the bumble bee which doesn't know that it is engineered in such a way that it shouldn't be able to fly at all! Anita Roddick the owner/founder of Body Shop again:

> A great advantage I had when I started the Body Shop was that I had never been to Business School. As I didn't know how things were supposed to be done I didn't know the rules and didn't know the risks. What is wonderful about the Body Shop is that we still don't know the rules.

Sometimes active dissatisfaction with how things are done in the organization still isn't enough to overcome inertia and create momentum for change. Although no successful business wants to get into the habit of reacting to crisis rather than gradual proactive change, recognizing or even creating the perception of a crisis can sometimes be the only way of getting a radical shift in attitude towards the need for change. Take, for example, the August *coup* in the USSR in 1990, when the military made an abortive attempt on power. The *coup* failed because of serious dissatisfaction within the upper echelons of the armed forces and a huge surge in active resistance on the streets of Moscow and Leningrad. However, as *The Economist* said at the time: 'failure of the *coup* has done what a year of negotiation had only promised, made inevitable the transformation of the Soviet political system.' The mere fact that the *coup* took place moved the world irrevocably on. It liberated forces in Soviet society which, for good or evil, can never be put back into Pandora's box. Similarly the failed *coup* in Spain, whether natural or engineered, when some top army colonels rose against King Juan Carlos, actually provided the opportunity for a reaffirmation of royalty and a check on military power. There could be no turning back the clock.

Sometimes it takes crisis or, at the very least, a new perspective in the form of a new role, or a new situation or a new place to dislocate us forcibly from our comfortable attachment to an easy life and propel us forward on a journey where the future is unknown and the past no longer accessible. Take, for example, the trauma of redundancy which, although an immensely painful and difficult crisis to handle, can sometimes provide the opportunity for developing a completely new and more satisfactory life direction. In their excellent pamphlet *Coping with redundancy*, the career counselling people of KPMG trace the transition stages through which someone will typically pass in adjusting to redundancy: from initial relief, to shock, searching, anger, self-doubt, acceptance, testing options, searching for new meaning and renewal. They include quotes from the partners of those who have survived redundancy which provide some hope that the painful destabilization of their lives has actually created new options which could not have existed before:

- 'An unusual chance for him to look at possible alternatives as a career and for us to re-evaluate the important things in our life, to make radical changes in our lives and to stop thinking of a job as total existence.'

- 'It would have been much harder to leave his old career had he not been made redundant – the redundancy gave him the opportunity he had been waiting for.'

Sometimes the destabilizing factors which free individuals up for the possibility of change are circumstantial, for example, losing one's job, or forming a new relationship, or even just going through the unsettling process of putting a house up for sale. All these factors create opportunities for change and by the sheer fact that they have happened inevitably move us on. Sometimes the 'crisis' which precipitates a change can be a sudden illumination or mind-set switch, as in the case of Terry Cooke-Davies, proprietor of Human Systems. Terry remembers the day when he woke up in the south of England to find trees and forests decimated by the storms of 1989. He says that as he looked around the ruin of trees which were 200 years old or more, yet had been felled in an instant, he vowed to give up his quest for stability and security, which were clearly illusory, and take the risk of setting up the business he'd always wanted to run.

The lesson for organizational change is that moving people out of their comfort zone can be a way of opening up the possibility of change. In this category might come encouraging career moves where managers work in other departments, other businesses, other countries, thus allowing new mind-sets and promoting a more open attitude towards change. Traditionally, the outward-bound leadership trust training experiences were just such a way of removing managers temporarily from their normal environment and by putting them in a completely unfamiliar situation – pot-holing, canoeing or leading an expedition across Dartmoor – challenging their assumptions and facilitating behavioural change.

Individual behaviour is powerfully shaped by the organizational roles that people play. Behaviour changes not because you issue an edict demanding that people 'be' different but because you give people new things to do and therefore to succeed they have to behave differently. The secret of managing and surviving change lies not so much in being different, as in shifting traditional roles, places, people and paradigms which, in itself, will open us up to the possibility of change.

EXERCISE 8

GUIDELINES TO STIMULATING DISSATISFACTION

The following checklist lets you assess whether you have the organizational mechanisms in place to air grievances, unfreeze old attitudes and challenge mind-sets.

Guidelines for organizational assessment

	Yes	No	Needs action
1. External threat • We have mechanisms to make us aware of enemy activity and external threats • We have regular data on customer competitive activities • We expose everyone to customers			
2. Self-criticism • Our appraisal system, management style and reward systems encourage continuous self-assessment and striving for improvement			
3. Attitude surveys • We conduct regular surveys of staff attitudes to 'benchmark' year-on-year performance and flag up areas of dissatisfaction			
4. Open management style • We encourage people to express critical views without seeing them as a negative attitude			
5. Recruit mavericks • We tolerate rebels, non-conformists and prophets of doom in the business			

6. Forum for airing grievances
   • We have regular cross-functional meetings to
     diagnose problems (i.e. quality circles/think-tanks/
     suggestion boxes/project teams)

7. Putting people in new situations
   • We have methods for encouraging people out of
     their comfort zones to do something different, i.e.
     career moves to other countries/businesses,
     secondments to other companies, new training
     situations, new roles

8. External consultants
   • We use external consultants to provide an objective
     view of the business

9. Creating a crisis
   • If necessary, we are prepared to engineer a 'crisis'

8.7 Summary

Active dissatisfaction and discontent with the status quo are part of
creating the dynamic of change. This means stimulating habits of
criticism and open debate, encouraging the expression of dissonant
views and even engineering a crisis. Organizations need rebels and
mavericks who point out that the emperor has no clothes on.
Glasnost, the open style, brings dissatisfaction to the surface and
fuels change. Challenging the status quo and breaking the rules are
an essential part of innovation and mean going in the opposite
direction to everyone else. Dislocating us from the comfortable past
can force our thinking outside the 'box' of routine patterns and free
us up for the possibility of change. Similarly, moving ourselves out
of the 'comfort zone' into new jobs, new countries, new teams can
shift our perspective and create opportunity for change. Does your
organization encourage people to take the risk of saying what they
think?

9

Communicate like crazy

For change to be sustainable, irreversible, it has to be rooted in many people in the organization. Somehow we have to achieve 'critical mass'. This chapter looks at a vital element of our change process: spreading change and gaining widespread involvement, creating a ripple effect across the organization. This means empowerment, a very topical issue for the 1990s. However, even though openness is purported to be a key value in many corporate cultures, managers don't understand what it means or how to do it. They are frightened of communicating. Fundamental dilemmas include:

- Do I communicate change top-down or bottom-up?
- Does consultation mean abdication?
- Do I withhold information until I know all the answers?
- If they have information, do they also have the power to refuse to do what I want?
- Shall I announce change as a *fait accompli* or live with the uncertainty and ambiguity of letting people know that I haven't got all the answers?

9.1 Information: the antidote to uncertainty

The essence of change is the move from the known to the unknown. Periods of crisis and of transition are always risky. The inherent ambiguity and uncertainty of change means that open, active and truthful communications lie at the heart of success. The more and the faster you are trying to change, the more openness you will need. It is interesting that if breakdown of communications is cited as the most common reason for divorce, it is also the most common reason for the failure of change programmes in organizations. 'More information' is the usual cry. How often does one hear of an organization that over-communicates? Special effort will be needed to pump information up, down and across the business. Moving information to people – the primary role of IT today – is paramount: not only to ownership and empowerment at a local level, but in integrating fragmented bits of the organization and allowing you to respond quickly to change, regardless of geographical constraints and time barriers.

Information is power to the people, information is control over your own destiny, information is understanding why change is necessary, information is the antidote to fear. Open communications mean that you can express your doubts about the change and even more important that you can understand and own the change rather than merely feeling it is being done to you.

9.2   What to communicate when ambiguity abounds

All very well, but as usual in management there is a dilemma. What are you actually supposed to be communicating? Suppose the change involves a merger or acquisition, there may be very little you can say about it at the planning stage. Even if there is no need for secrecy, then, as the initiator of change, you may be hard-pressed to answer the very detailed questions people have for you: 'When will it happen?' 'Who will be affected?' 'How?' 'Specifically, in what ways?' The trouble is that there is no great blueprint in the sky and you probably don't know the answers either! In fact, if you try to pin down the uncertainties too much you will actually paralyze action and stop the change happening at all. It's like having a planeload of passengers sitting on the runway at Heathrow. Everyone knows that the destination is Zurich, but now the passengers are demanding that you, the pilot, tell them: the weather en route, where and when they will get air sick, the precise route you will be flying and the exact time of arrival at the passport desk.

Clearly, some of these factors are outside your control, others are at present unknown and unknowable. The analogy of the journey of change is a useful one. It indicates that although you can, and should, spell out the direction and destination of change, you cannot yet know the actual route and details of the journey, because these will change as you go along.

As a frequent and probably disillusioned traveller you will know that there is nothing more frustrating than an unexplained plane delay: four hours of silence. Even bad news, or an announcement that there is no news yet, is better than nothing at all. At least if you know that nothing is going to happen for the next hour, you can go and get a coffee, ring the office or buy that best-seller. Communication, even if you don't know all the facts, at least demonstrates that you recognize people's insecurity and are trying to be open. It is the sense of helplessness and lack of control over one's own destiny which infuriates us all about communication blackouts.

Sometimes it seems as though managers are terrified of the truth and feel that they have to be mealy-mouthed in protecting employees from something they cannot be trusted to understand.

The redundant manager

A multinational, which prided itself on its open and honest style, carried out a reorganization which involved making a very senior and well-respected manager redundant. The whole issue obviously embarrassed them. A memo was sent round explaining the new structure, but making no mention whatsoever of the disappearance of the director. As several employees said afterwards: 'It was as if he had never existed, as if he were dead.' For all his sins, or lack of them, the man was well known and many people resented his summary treatment. And yet no one argued against the fact that redundancies, unpleasant as they are, are a fact of life which have to be faced. Was it really so impossible to acknowledge the director's past contribution, thank him for what he had achieved and wish him every success in the future? This was all it took.

It's all so unnecessary. Most of us are sadly familiar with business or personal overdrafts and have long ago discovered one simple fact of life – keeping the bank manager informed in advance of a problem is an essential part of managing the relationship. No one likes nasty surprises which come out of the blue. So it is in any dynamic business; while you may not be able to communicate all that people would like, you can at least open the channels for regular and honest dialogue and talk about your intentions. Don't be put off communicating because you don't know all the answers, some of your staff may already have guessed that you don't walk on water. Waiting too long before you involve people is usually a fatal mistake. Why not involve people early in talking about the problem, putting together a 'strawman' with some key players which, with further debate, will become a 'tinman' and finally an 'ironman'. It's a dangerous illusion to suppose that even the apparently obvious candidates for secrecy, such as redundancies and takeovers, cannot be handled more openly.

An open and shut case?

- The *Financial Times* reporting on BTR's acquisition of Hawker Siddeley, points out that within days of the bid victory, every Hawker MD and FD was summoned to a Heathrow hotel to hear about BTR's plans for Hawker. As the CEO Robert Faircloth said at the time, 'A key is to create a sense of urgency very quickly.' A 'minder', counsellor or godfather was allocated to each significant Hawker manager to get closer to the people and the business.

- A manufacturing unit of ICL in Sydenham went into communications overkill to discuss its plans for redundancy and closure two years in advance of the fact. Far from losing production and people, the rundown was achieved with full productivity and attendance up to the very day of closure.

- Robert Segesser the owner and founder of Dairyborn Foods (turnover in 1991, £5 million) reported to the *Daily Telegraph* in 1991 that after much pain and acrimony he had finally, with the help of '3i', bought out his partner. During this traumatic period he had talked very little to his workforce, describing himself honestly as a bit too 'cavalier' and 'gung ho'. For quite a while it left a nasty taste in their mouth. As a successful entrepreneur, standing up in front of his workforce to explain bad – or for that matter good – news was not Robert's favourite activity. But now he thinks it pays.

9.3   Glasnost: the open style

Earlier we looked at the implications of four different management styles for handling change: artisan, meddler, hero and strategist.

Each has a distinctive way of communicating change. The artisan, into which box we might temporarily put Robert Segesser, is typical of the early start-up phase of business growth when the owner/ founder *is* the business and is too busy doing to be bothered with communicating. The number of people employed is small, everyone works together in one portakabin or one factory unit, informal communications are easy, and the whole team can easily fit around the bar billiards table in the pub. Robert himself admits that he hasn't bothered too much with meetings and briefing groups. He was, of necessity, more used to rolling up his sleeves and getting on with the job himself. The artisan communicates on an *ad hoc*, informal basis. He might just about run to an occasional management meeting, but tends only to communicate at moments of crisis – which, of course, are usually moments of bad news. The peril of this style of communicating is that it places all the load on one person and doesn't build any willingness for change from others. It can also mean that there is very little positive internal PR.

The meddler has a high anxiety level and low trust, communications are a method of control for keeping your finger on the pulse of the business, the communications are closed rather than open. When to dot the i's and cross the t's is his concern. The meddler is a worrier, frightened things are getting out of control. Communications mean being there, they're primarily top-down, characterized by 1-to-1 communications, different messages to different people and a lot of memos flying in all directions. There is a story about Russell Seal, chief executive of BP Oil, who was known, in typical BP 'command and control' style, for the frequency and incisiveness of his 'blue' memos, the arrival of which would strike fear into his managers' hearts. As part of his personal role in creating change he agreed that he would stop sending his missives – although he readily admitted that he couldn't promise he would stop writing them! The trouble with the meddlesome style of communicating change is that it loses out on the process of transferring ownership and responsibility to the team. Given that communication of change should be tight/loose (the loose being local freedom to operate without referral upwards) the meddler is literally uptight. Desire for control when it seems to be slipping away is an understandable motivator of this kind of behaviour, although it doesn't help root the change. Sometimes massive culture change programmes fall into the paradox of 'You will participate and own change . . . and here's how'.

The hero is a natural communicator, good on his or her feet, effective in getting the message across. Frequently, the hero will get a 'high' from his or her 'state of the nation' addresses, brainstorming meetings, roadshows, self-starring videos or management briefings. It's all something of an ego trip. Meetings are carefully scripted and equally carefully recorded. Question and answer notes are kept. And very useful the hero can be too at times of crisis on Greiner's chart, when someone needs to stand at the top of the organization with a loudspeaker delivering a rallying cry to the troops. Typically the hero is a god-like figure: revered, hated or feared. His ego can make him very paranoid about receiving any organization criticism which he can interpret personally. If he receives questions in this light not surprisingly they will rapidly dry up; to a god each question is a proving ground for his leadership.

For communicating change, particularly in periods of steady growth rather than crisis (evolution rather than revolution), research shows that an open, two-way style of communication is the most effective in guaranteeing lasting and irreversible change. The strategist doesn't need a carefully scripted event, he or she can cope with the impromptu. What will be remarkable in the business will be the sheer amount of talking and debate going on and the openness with which views are expressed without fear: the courage around the organization to speak about shortcomings, errors and difficulties. The strategist will certainly be setting and communicating the vision and values in many ways, but he or she will also be doing a lot of listening and networking. The strategist's face will be turned both to outward communications and inward communications, particularly symbolic events such as presentations, informal get-togethers and induction programmes.

Openness also means that honesty is the best policy when communicating change, even when the change is of crisis proportions. It rarely pays to tell lies in business or in private life, if only because of the danger of getting caught in the act. Contrast, for example, the handling of two very similar crises both involving the global withdrawal of a major brand. The first was Johnson & Johnson's withdrawal of its painkiller Tylenol in 1986 when, for the second time, some capsules were deliberately contaminated with cyanide. The second crisis was when, in early 1990, traces of benzene were found in bottles of Perrier water. J & J apparently panicked briefly and then took itself back to its famous corporate credo, which reminded the organization of its long-held values of openness, ethical behaviour and integrity. The disaster was dealt with in a straightforward, honest way, even though the health risks were far worse than in the case of Perrier. The French company, on the other hand, blew it. Their response was as damaging as the original contamination. They broke every rule in the book – they played the problem down, they claimed, on no evidence at all, that contamination was limited to the North American bottling line and then discovered, less than three days later, the real cause: contamination at the Vergèze plant in France. The firm had to change its story. Because Perrier fumbled its initial explanations so badly it got a rotten press worldwide. Pure water perhaps, but certainly not pure communications. This one piece of communication – or lack of it – cost the chairman and founder his job and has had a bitter legacy in Perrier's devalued shares and vulnerability to takeover.

Many managers feel that they cannot afford to be open and honest for fear of hurting people or embarrassing themselves. In the Prudential Assurance Company, for example, the aspect of change which most worries middle managers is communicating bad news. As every change inevitably involves an element of bad as well as good news, it's very important to bite the bullet and not disguise the reality of the situation. In the absence of information, people will invent far worse scenarios for themselves than you can ever do. (Look again at the brownie points which the Liberal Democrat leader, Paddy Ashdown, scored in admitting to the truth of the rumour of a past indiscretion.)

9.4   The $64,000 question: how?

Communicating the vision, the destination, the 'why' of change is important, but in the end, most of us are more interested to know 'how' the change will affect us. As the pace of change hots up in the 1990s, more and more organizations are getting in touch with the environment and seeing the writing on the wall. We probably know why we should change and even what we should change, but when it comes to how we're going to do it, well, there's the rub! Just reiterating the 'why' tends to get people agitated into a cycle of confusion: they're all dressed up with nowhere to go.

Translating the 'why' into 'how'

When ICL set up its business centres the 'why' eventually made total sense, the trouble was that no one knew how to make it work. While John Davison, manager of the prototype Retail Business Centre, was deputed to come back to the top team with a blueprint for action, the rest of the Business Centre managers struggled to learn by experiment and example. Some of the 'hows' with which they wrestled were:

- How to track many small products when previously they had only a few large mainframes.
- How to measure product-line profitability across product, geographic and industry dimensions.
- How to deal with peer group managers who get confrontational about challenging input to the P & L.

When Komatsu decided to take out Caterpillar – the vision – the war cry was devastatingly clear. But the skill of the CEO was that every 2 to 3 years he could translate the 'why' into a series of steps or slogans, for example, 'reliability', or 'cost saving' or 'quality'.

9.5 'Top-down' or 'bottom-up'?

Change imposed top-down just doesn't work. Grassroots change is the only assurance of the irreversibility of the process. This presents senior managers with yet another paradox – directing a 'non-directive' change programme. This doesn't mean that the manager has no role to play; to some extent change must be simultaneously a revolution from above and from below. You cannot change an entire organization unless the people at the top support and are committed to the change. Put another way, the 'top-down' initiative is vital but should content itself with the general direction in which the company should move, without insisting on specific solutions. After all, it's a rare CEO who knows in advance the fine-grained details of how organization change will work in the diverse units of a large corporation.

Effective corporate renewal starts at the bottom through informal efforts to solve business problems. It also usually starts at the periphery, on the sidelines of the organization, led by general managers of those units, rather than the CEO or staff people. Effective change is about solving concrete business problems more than it is about abstractions such as 'culture change' or 'participation'.

Gorbachev and the failure of the 'top-down' approach

Gorbachev's passionate attempts for perestroika are a case in point: 'We have tried to do too much from above, it doesn't work.' One can feel immense sympathy for the man. 'We only thought we were in the saddle, whilst the actual situation was that the automobile was not going where the one at the steering wheel thought it was going.' He began to try to merge the initiative from above with the grassroots movement from below, stating that 'the weaknesses and inconsistencies of all known revolutions from above are explained precisely through the lack of such support from below'. However, he left it too late. *The Economist* in March 1991 reported that 'during the second half of last year his method of reforming from the top down reached its logical limit. It clashed with the forces he himself had unleashed, those demanding change from the bottom up.' Nemesis followed swiftly. The collapse of the *coup* against him in August 1991 was a magnificent demonstration of grassroots opinion. The 'three days that shook the world' were followed in quick succession by Gorbachev's reluctant disbanding of communism, the break-up of the USSR and his own political demise.

9.6   Ownership and early involvement

Amazing things happen when people take responsibility for changing things themselves. The results are quite different and at times people are unrecognizable. Their work changes and at the same time their attitude to it. The examples may seem small but they add up to something impressive, switching on the light bulb of people power, empowerment for real. One manager recently told an everyday story about ringing a car rental firm to hire a car for an urgent Brussels–London return trip. He was in London at the time and therefore rang the London office. A young woman told him that the deal could only be set up from Brussels. As he was about to put the telephone down in disgust, he realized that she was still talking to him, telling him that she would solve the problem and ring him back within half an hour. A likely story! But she did. She couldn't have been more than eighteen but in her book she was a professional, there to solve the customer problem. The initiative was hers and she took it.

Real ownership comes when people think it is their change and

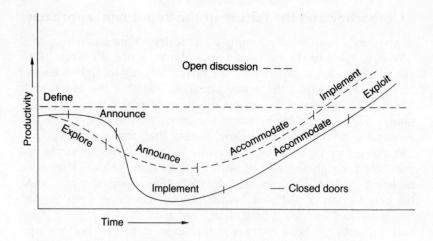

Figure 9.1   Early involvement pays off

not yours. It means getting over the psychology of dependence which says: 'This is none of our business, let the bosses have the headache.'

People who feel that they have an element of control over their own destiny are much more likely to be willing to change. Early involvement, as anyone who has ever worked in a project team will know, also increases the sense of ownership and commitment and is more likely to create critical mass for the change and reduce resistance. Early involvement means investment at the beginning of the change curve. Figure 9.1 shows that although it will initially take more time and effort, the potential pay-offs are enormous in flattening the depth of the productivity decline and speeding up emergence into productivity gains.

Managers sit behind closed doors. They spend painful hours defining and honing their plans for change and then they announce them to an astounded world. It's a 'macho' approach, which says: 'Only we could have created this. Aren't we clever? You'd better get on and do it.' The announcement of the change rarely coincides with its reality. Productivity plummets as people's resistance soars and their ingenuity in wriggling out of 'yet another change' reasserts itself. Eventually they accommodate the change, or prove, yet again, that if you keep your head down the change will go away.

By contrast, open discussion means taking much longer in the early stages to explore the issues with key players and get their input. But, of course, it means that your levels of frustration may rise; it also means that your plans for change will change as they go along, and so will you. However, the pay-off is that by the time you announce the change you are announcing something that is well on its way. It's the braver, wiser and more self-confident choice of approaches.

Although the words 'empowerment' and 'consultation' are every-day currency, few of us really know what they mean in practice. This creates a potential credibility gap in managing change because it often translates into managers paying lip-service to consulting people about change when they have already decided what to do and don't intend to listen at all. Change is then seen as a *fait accompli* and the managers' mock consultation is revealed for what it is. It is absolutely vital in any piece of communication to decide in advance what are the 'givens', the non-negotiable pieces of the change which are not open to debate. One BP director described this empower-ment dilemma very neatly when he put forward the analogy of a swimming pool. You can't 'empower' people to swim freely, he said, until you have drawn the boundaries which constitute the pool, and put them not in murky water, but in a clear element through which they can see their way and move.

Having consulted at least the key players, well in advance and with honesty, the change manager starts to create his 'strawmen', 'tinmen', 'ironmen'. He involves others in defining the change and is not deterred by the intrinsic messiness of the process. How about when the time comes to let everyone know about the change? As well as the possibility of some kind of general announcement through formal communication channels, the change manager will want to talk individually with each of the people involved in the change. Most managers know this, but it is how they do what they do that causes the problems, as illustrated by these comments:

- 'Communication was like a dentist's waiting room – Next. – My interview took all of six minutes.'
- 'I wanted space for reflection, to think it through and come back a day or two later, but I wasn't allowed this time.'
- 'No one really checked my understanding and yet this is such a vital and continuous requirement in change management.'
- 'I was told: "These are the changes, how do you feel – good, well I'm sure you'll cope"!'

The lessons are strikingly simple. Achieving 'buy-in' to change means giving people freely the gift of your time and genuinely

sten. It means knowing your people as whole human
, families, interests, agendas outside the immediate work
nt. It means communicating in chunks – telling people a
litt.   ing them time to think about it and arranging for them to
come back to you. It means constantly checking and rechecking
understanding.

9.7   Establishing communication channels

If you are coping with a high and continuous rate of change, it is
probable that you will need to invent new methods of communicating, as well as more fully using the old methods. What is needed is
a whole raft of group and individual communications, formal and
informal processes which you are constantly assessing and revamping. Even if you are one of the lucky managers to whom the human
touch comes naturally, you will, as the business grows, want to put
mechanisms in place to do this on a regular, systematic basis up,
down and across the organization. Formal communication channels
are needed to avoid 'casualties' and ensure that everyone knows
everything they need to know. In one company, while a group
announcement of change was taking place, the girl on the reception
desk was found in floods of tears – no one had thought to involve
her!

Getting the change message down through the organization is
much less problematic in a business start-up where you all share the
same values and vision, work and go to the pub together. Typically,
as the business moves up the Greiner growth curve, cracks appear,
parts of the organization splinter, new blood dilutes the original
'feel', there are too many people all to fit on one donkey on the
beach at Scarborough (Croda International, now with a £375 million
turnover, in 1924 had just six people and was actually so photo-
graphed – the photograph's on display at their head office in
Cowick).

In large organizations the problem will be made worse by the
inheritance of a traditional hierarchical structure, with layers of
management which can act like soggy cotton wool, soaking up and
distorting the message from the top.

Somehow you will have to unclog the arteries and get the
communication flow going, whether it's by:

- Industrial Society-type 'cascade' briefing groups.
- Robb Wilmot's 'robbograms', mission statements, 'ICL Way' values statements, videos.
- Ford hiring the Royal Albert Hall to address dealer principals on the launch of a new marque.
- 'State of the nation' addresses by the CEO, perhaps twice yearly.

The key to downwards communication is to make it little and often and face to face, to ensure that even at this stage there is a two-way exchange of views – part of creating the early involvement. It is extraordinary that so many managers bemoan the fact that after time-consuming and laborious attempts on their part to communicate, they get no response, no feedback and no questions – just a sea of dispirited faces and a deafening silence. Of course, when you create the right circumstances, man, being a gregarious animal, will feel free to talk. It won't happen on its own; people will be too inhibited, particularly in a large group. After a piece of downward communication you may need to split into smaller groups, using 'facilitators' if it helps, and trying to encourage discussion this way.

However, there is more to communicating change than just funnelling it down through the organization. Modern businesses need communication and feedback up the organization and increasingly across it too as functional barriers break down and horizontal production flows take over. It is this free exchange of ideas across the business which is intrinsic to creativity and change.

Formalizing the informal

Jim Treybig, who founded Tandem Computers in 1974, has built a $1.6 billion turnover business with 10,000 employees worldwide. Tandem are famous for wanting to preserve the informal, family-feel team culture which arose from those early Silicon Valley days in the back of someone's garage. Even their annual accounts give a team feel. But how to preserve a small company culture when you have become a huge multinational? Tandem have institutionalized what they originally called 'beer busts', now renamed in these puritanical days of the 1990s 'peanut parties'. Everywhere in the world – Frankfurt, London or Cupratino – work stops at 3 p.m. on a Friday afternoon and everyone – customers, family, friends – gather informally around the pool table just to talk and to have some fun and unwind before the weekend. It is an act of faith. If you are running a training programme in Dusseldorf you will kindly but firmly be informed that when the clock strikes three you're welcome to join the party but otherwise you're on your own!

Thomas Allen, a professor at MIT, has studied communication patterns and arrived at the less than startling conclusion that people talk to each other more when they work in close proximity. Workers on different floors, or even different sides of the 'open-plan' divides, may as well be in a different building, so rarely do they talk to each other. According to *The Economist* 'the eternal coffee break' will transform offices into social centres, 'neighbourhoods' where marketing/manufacturing/design people can be located close to each other and where top management will live in a cluster of offices wrapped around the atrium in the middle of the building.

9.8 Ten commandments for getting it wrong

Here is a list of some of the things to avoid if you want your communication channels to stay open:

1. Criticize your predecessor: he or she screwed up.
2. Don't tell anyone anything until you've spelt out the last detail.
3. Tell lies.
4. Impose a communications blackout.
5. Announce a change, then try to get it to work.
6. Time major changes for the Friday afternoon before Christmas.
7. Be autocratic: Genghis Khan didn't consult.
8. Discourage people from criticizing the status quo and saying what they think, you might not like the answers.
9. Rely on memos: talking is a waste of time.
10. Don't forget it's your change not theirs.

EXERCISE 9

AN AUDIT OF YOUR COMMUNICATIONS PACKAGE

In 'auditing' your existing communications package it's worth reviewing the headings given below to ensure that you have a good mix of mechanisms. You don't need all of them but you do need to check that you are not relying too heavily on only one or two. For example, it's all too easy to think that well-conducted briefing groups are the answer to everything. Do they really provide an opportunity for free, open, two-way discussions? Do they address the issue of cross-fertilization across functions and businesses? Are they, in fact, a remnant of our old hierarchical thinking?

Similarly, too many of us think that electronic mail solves the communication problem, whereas frequently it is information gone mad, overload without meaning. What about the irreplacable method of face-to-face contact, individually or in teams, formally and informally? Are we forgetting that we are the master and technology only an enabler?

Audit checklist
Please put a √ for OK, a X for not applicable and a ? for worth considering.

Cascade team briefings on a regular basis ☐
Management by walkabout ☐
Beer busts/happy hours/informal get-togethers ☐
Networking ☐
Regular management meetings, say, monthly ☐
Twice yearly, 'state of the nation' addresses ☐
Roadshows/presentations to other parts of the organization ☐
Monthly '1-on-1s' with key managers ☐
Project teams, taskforces: multilevel multidisciplinary ☐
'Awaydays' brainstorm sessions around a flip-chart ☐
Electronic mail ☐
Video conferencing to cut down international travel ☐
Think-tanks/Quality circles ☐
Steering groups, working parties ☐
Parties, celebrations, hoopla ☐
Mentors/godfathers/minders ☐
Exit interviews: why are people leaving? ☐
Attitude surveys to open the can of worms ☐
Office layout/eating arrangements conducive to social contact ☐
Company magazines, videos, etc. ☐
Birthday breakfasts/informal lunches with a selection of staff ☐
Cross-boundary problem-solving groups ☐

9.9 Summary

Active and open communication is the antidote to the uncertainty of change. The more dynamic your business environment the more you will need to communicate and keep communicating. The change manager must overdose on communications. It's said that you can't be too thin or too rich; equally you can't have too much communication. Lack of communication is the most frequently cited reason for the failure of change programmes. Top-down, unilaterally imposed change doesn't work. You need bottom-up change, early involvement and genuine consultation. A raft of communications channels, both group and individual, formal and informal, will be essential. It may be worth carrying out a quick audit of your own communication channels to ensure that the lines are open.

10

Time, timing and transition

One of the great challenges of sustaining organization change is to find an answer to the paradox of time. The external marketplace, the shareholders, the City want change *now*, but this isn't the reality of how organizations work. Except in times of crisis, and sometimes not even then, instant change is rarely sustainable change. The dilemma is expressed in the continuing saga of Lloyds of London. There are signs of change, but they're not coming fast enough for many of the 'names' whose money is at stake. The managing agents of the many small syndicates are in a cleft stick, they are being harassed by the 'names' and yet the body of Lloyds isn't changing fast enough for them to demonstrate they are listening and responding to their customers.

Opportunities in the marketplace will always present themselves randomly to any business organization. Whether the business can take advantage of them depends on its internal capability to manage change fast and effectively. Because by the time a crisis arrives it is probably too late, this means that through the 1990s organizations need to be in a continuous state of readiness to react to whatever is thrown at them. The length of time between the 'environment' lobbing the ball and the organization returning the shot becomes a vital part of competitive edge. Speeding up the response time is the challenge. The way of doing it is ironically through incremental change, a mind-set of gradual and continuous small shifts.

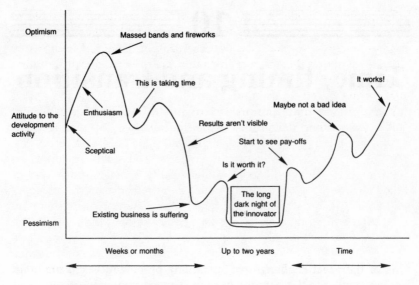

Source: Philipp and Dunlop

Figure 10.1 The long dark night of the innovator

10.1 Change takes longer than you think

We consistently underestimate the time it takes to get change to happen. Think how long we mull over and 'incubate' changes in our personal lives: a job or career change, even planning a holiday! Typically in organizations managers assume that change will happen overnight and are rarely sensitive to the in-built delays and the dangers of being impatient. It is critically important that management acknowledge and consider carefully the lead-time for change to bear results.

Unfortunately, the inevitable fall-off in production which results from any change increases the likelihood that managers who have an unrealistic expectation of how long change will take to achieve will panic and pull the plug on the change just when they are about to start to see the pay-off. This phenomenon is well described by John Philipp and Sandy Dunlop, adapting an idea from Darryl Connor and depicting it as 'the long dark night of the innovator' (Figure 10.1).

Figure 10.1 is a development of the 'productivity curve' we introduced in Chapter 4, which demonstrates the inevitable fall-off in productivity when change occurs. It is instantly recognizable to most managers. The stage of 'massed bands and fireworks', which heralds major programmes of organization change, is horribly familiar, whether it be a reorganization, culture change, programme of total quality management or a huge systems change. So is the fact that having raised expectation, absolutely nothing seems to happen for a very long time. Enthusiasm dwindles, cynicism spreads that this is yet another 'flavour of the month' initiative, top management starts to back away from what increasingly looks like a failure, the change is aborted and eventually something else will be launched with another fanfare of doom. What results is layer upon layer of failed changes, each experience increasing the cynicism of managers and staff. It is exactly like a gardener who, having planted his new seedlings waits only a matter of days before pulling them up by the roots to see how they are doing.

Everything looks like a failure half-way through. It takes courage to stay with a change during this period, to persevere, to maintain enthusiasm and commitment.

ABC Retail and pulling the plug on change

ABC Retail is part of an American consumer chain. It has been established in the United Kingdom for some 70 years, where it employs over 2,000 staff in almost 150 branches. In 1988 a new French chief executive was appointed. His job was to implement a vast programme of change, moving the organization from formal traditional values towards greater delegation of authority levels and greater personal responsibility. He said it would take time. In 1990, the shareholders, concerned about low profits, forced him out. A CEO was brought over from the United States to undo the changes made by his predecessor and to 'bring the UK operation back into the family'.

Quite apart from the lost productivity, the unnecessary aggravation for nothing, this kind of 'stop/go' approach to change has had enormous costs in terms of company morale. Many had identified strongly with the charisma and intent of the French CEO, who for good reasons had introduced the teddy bear as a kind of organizational symbol and mascot. Apparently after he had been sacked and the American mafia arrived back on the scene, there were ritual burnings, a pogrom against any teddy bear unwise enough to show himself. The employees now say that top management has no credibility with them whatsoever, that they cannot believe a word they say.

Change always takes longer than you think. For example, it has been estimated that it takes at least 3–5 years for any major programme of strategic change or attitude shift to become truly part of a company's persona. One or two of the big and extremely prestigious Swedish banks have privately admitted that it has taken them many years to turn such unwieldy organizations around. One bank felt that it had taken them the best part of 19 years, since 1972, to achieve a fast and comprehensive de-centralized response to the market.

Even in a small responsive business, the temptation is to assume that change can be made to happen overnight. For example, one chief executive we know asked his consultant to deliver a totally new culture and to have it in place by the next Board meeting! The risk of not allowing sufficient time for the change to 'bed down' is that the embryo change plant will be pulled up and thrown on the rubbish heap, to be succeeded by yet another change and another after that – all equally likely to meet the same fate. So the change process predictably takes time, costs money and effort, and causes an immediate fall-of in productivity.

There is a great trap in pushing for productivity too soon. Everyone seems sure that 'in time' Russia will change, but those words capture much truth and conceal much nastiness. For years to come there will be tensions in a dying empire, more economic dislocation, probably a lot more fighting. However, there is a big dilemma here. It takes time for people to work their way through the process of change from shock, through denial to acknowledgement, adaptation and finally, change. But there isn't any time – the market frequently doesn't allow much leeway. The challenge, therefore, is to find ways of shortcircuiting or speeding up the process.

10.2   Evolutionary v. revolutionary change

As Greiner illustrates, all organizations go through periods of both evolution and revolution. Sometimes it's difficult to implement change at all in the absence of a crisis. Sometimes, as we've seen, we may even need to engineer the 'crisis'. At the same time, Greiner's model argues for proactive rather than reactive change – anticipating the next crisis rather than waiting until the shock-waves hit. Revolutions have the advantage of speed. Typically in businesses, they take the form of abrupt reorganizations. These drastic shifts are traumatic in terms of human costs and even worse, although they appear to be quick and efficient, this may well be illusory, masking a response which says, 'Let's keep our head down until the pressure goes away, and then revert to business as usual.'

Evolutionary or gradual change is much more productive – a sequence of changes rather than a sudden reorganization. But this process of change can be very slow. As we've said, it's important to speed up the ability to respond to change, otherwise the market 'windows' for which the business is trying to change will have long since disappeared.

10.3   Lead-times and change tools

We're used to the concept of lead-time in getting a product to market. Lead-times in managing change are just as significant to the business. Shorter lead-times make quicker change and greater competitive edge. Time-lags are important barriers to change, created by both perception-lags when people are unable or unwilling to recognize the need for change and action-lags when nothing happens even though the problem may have been recognized intellectually and even though senior management thinks they've pulled the right levers.

Perception-lags occur when the organization fails to recognize the need for change, sometimes because it is doggedly following the recipes for past success, sometimes because it is so fragmented that there is no way of formulating a coherent perception of the external environment.

It's amazing the extent to which people in business believe that there is an objective reality, yet it is *how* people see things, right or wrong, which will influence whether they change or not. We can choose to see the world in new ways. The breakthrough to overcoming perception-lags lies in education.

Action-lags occur because people's hearts and minds don't necessarily follow each other. Intellectual agreement has no consequences unless managers' self-interest and the balance of power are aligned. If not, the battle between rationality and raw emotion is all too often won by the latter.

We can change procedures and make new proposals quickly and easily, but it is the personal views of key managers that will determine whether a change plan is actively killed or propelled towards corporate approval. Therefore, it is critical for top management to acknowledge and consider carefully the lead-time for any mechanism to bear results.

Different change tools have different timeframes. A single executive change at the top of the organization will have a much quicker impact than reshaping the appraisal systems, changing career planning or introducing a new culture into the business. These changes can only be paced at the acceptance level of the managers who are being asked to make them happen.

10.4   Timing is all

Managing change means recognizing when the time is ripe for change or, as the Australian philosopher A. Cannon says, 'There is a tide in the affairs of men which taken at its ebb can turn into a real bastard!' Japanese managers are by reputation acutely aware of the importance of timing in business. Mark McCormack, the sports impresario, talks about planting the 'seed' for change in someone's mind by a telephone call to a tennis star, which although it resulted in an immediate rejection eventually bore fruit years later when the star himself approached McCormack to become part of his sports circus. Boris Yeltsin, talking of his days as a party boss in Moscow, said: 'Perhaps I made some mistakes. It wasn't what I said but when I said it.' Best of all is the wry comment of ex-President Bush after the Gulf crisis in August 1990 was followed by the Russian *coup* in August 1991: 'What is it about August?'

Just as timing is the secret of great theatre so it is the secret of successful change. Timing is to do with the state of readiness of the organization. Readiness for change exists at the point when there are neither very high security levels, nor very low security levels. If people are too insecure then they tend to dig in, retrench and resist change. When they are too secure – some of our famous insurance companies, for example – then there is equally no readiness. The time isn't right.

The right time depends on both the willingness and motivation for change and the capability to carry out the necessary task. Capability involves power, influence, authority and having the right resources, information and skills to do the job. A simple chart helps to assess both readiness and capability and is attached later as the chapter assignment.

10.5 Announcementitis: macho v. Zen

Everyone knows that to announce a change on a Friday afternoon, when people have a whole weekend to worry and telephone each other and invent little green men, is not a good idea, nor the day before Christmas. Nor is it all that sensible to have an annual gobbet of change imposed in 'October Revolution' fashion.

In fact, to announce a change at all may be a dangerous proposition. After all, as the old adage goes, 'there's many a slip 'twixt cup and lip.' You may be in danger of announcing what you have no guarantee will actually happen. Here's a cynical quote from a survey of a company where 'announcementitis' prevailed:

> All we have is slogans. Will $1 + 1 = 4$ next year? Let's turn slogans into reality. We think if you invent a buzz word and put people round it then you have done it right but it's not turned into anything real.

'Announcementitis' puts resistance sky high and yet it is probably still the most frequent method managers use to put a change across, often pinned on the noticeboard along the lines:

Friday 13th
Important Announcement to all Staff
As from Monday X Division will be moving to Scunthorpe and Y Division will stay in Knightsbridge. An organization chart is affixed, please take notice of your new responsibilities.
P.S. There are no car parking spaces available in Scunthorpe.

There are other ways of doing things, the 'Zen' rather than 'macho' approach, which is nicely described by Richard Pascale Tanner and Anthony G. Athos (1982) in the *Art of Japanese Management*:

> Instead of turning the spotlight on an intended change, parading organization charts and job descriptions, Americans might better consider reassigning tasks incrementally, gradually shifting boundaries between functions, instead of legislating a final change. This approach involves taking your intention to the key actors, perfecting your design by learning as you proceed.

It is said that the typical American style is to announce a change and then spend months and years trying to get it to work, whereas the Japanese put enormous early effort into researching the change, winning over the key players so that when the change is announced it has already started to happen, and they are merely announcing a developing reality.

10.6 Managing transition: creating time and space

The Japanese have a word 'ma', which literally means 'a space in time'. Managing transition successfully means providing the space to get used to leaving one situation and arriving at another. For example, consider leaving work in the evening. Some people might be delighted to snap their fingers and instantly translate themselves home. Most of us, however, quite welcome the journey time in the car or bus, or just having a pint in the pub. We need to switch off from one situation before we can relax into the home situation.

So it is with organizational change. Managers need to create a breathing space which allows people to plan and prepare, review where they've been and take stock of the future. Man is a very adaptive animal if only he is given the chance to get used to the idea. It's amazing how much change he can accept, but this will only happen if the manager, Atlas-like, keeps the organization pressures off the embryo change plant. The job of management is almost to create a 'bell jar' within which people are protected from the weight of the organization, which otherwise will demand too much productivity too early and will, by the sheer weight of its demands, stifle change.

As Sir Michael Edwardes once said: 'For change to be managed it has to be manageable.' This means breaking the change down into bite-sized chunks or, as the Americans, say: 'Don't put out more tomato plants than you can water.' Each stage of the change process will have its own mini-vision, because the whole process is an iterative one. It's possible to spell out in advance every step along the way. Bite-sized chunks of change means realistic, achievable goals. This gives the change credibility and the participants confidence in their abilities. Getting started may be difficult, but short-term intermediate goals make it easier to take the first step.

If change is to continue, once begun, it will need to be monitored and the momentum maintained. Small successes create the possibility of people catching themselves doing something right. Maintaining momentum means small and immediate rewards, creating role models of the people who are promoting the changed behaviour, being singled out by the organization, made visible and rewarded.

EXERCISE 10

ASSESSING READINESS AND CAPABILITY FOR CHANGE

Is the timing right for the change you are anticipating? Please complete the chart below for a quick assessment.

Readiness capability assessment chart

Individuals or groups critical to the change effort	Readiness			Capability		
	High	Medium	Low	High	Medium	Low
1.						
2.						
3.						
4.						
5.						
6.						

Source: After Beckhard and Harris (1987)

10.7 Summary

Change takes longer than you think. It's dangerous to assume that change will happen overnight. Being impatient with the in-built time-lags of change and pushing for productivity too soon can create unrealistic expectations and result in aborted change plans. There is an inherent dilemma. People need time to progress through the stages of the change process but market forces are rarely generous enough to allow this. Whereas revolutionary change appears instantaneous, the people costs can undermine an illusory efficiency. Evolutionary change – planned as a sequence of small steps – is frequently more effective in the long run. The more we can eliminate perception-lags, when people don't want to see the writing on the wall, and action-lags, because their hearts aren't in the change, the quicker we can get them through the process. A 'big bang' announcement may not be the best method. Timing is all. We must also provide a bubble of time and space in which the change can grow, protected from the weight of organization demands. Before we put together a plan for making change happen it's worth assessing the organization capability and state of readiness for change.

11

Making it happen

11.1 Are you convinced?

You are the key to managing and sustaining change. How convinced are you that it is a journey you want to make? Openness to change in your own personal and professional life means challenging old assumptions, getting out of the rut, avoiding the 'victim' stance and offering yourself up to the possibilities of the future. The fact that you actually feel the pain and discomfort of change is likely to make you a far more mature and sensitive guide to others whom you may be guiding through organizational change.

You job is to make change happen as fast as the external market place requires and as fast as the people you are managing can sustain. What are you going to do to move people through the predictable process of change as quickly and painlessly as possible?

11.2 Summary of key messages and challenges

Before you look at what actions you are going to take to make change happen, you may wish to refresh your memory on the key points which we have discussed in this book. A quick summary is given in Figure 11.1.

Challenges to you	Key messages from 'the essence of change'
	1. There is no alternative: change or die.
	2. There isn't a fault in reality so we must adjust our mind-set, challenge our old assumptions, reinvent ourselves. It can be exciting!
• What will the future look like and how will it make demands on your thinking?	3. Organizations are being transformed out of all recognition: their strategy, systems, structure, culture and people.
	4. Managing change effectively has become a vital part of competitive edge. You can get the environmental scanning bit right and still be boiled alive because you can't move people quickly enough to take advantage of market opportunities.
• When you pull the lever for change does anything happen?	5. The manager's job is to create the highest rate of change that the organization and people can sustain. This means managing people through the predictable stages of the change process as quickly and painlessly as possible. Change hurts; there are productivity and people costs. But the good news is that change is a predictable and therefore a manageable process, that understanding what you've gone through helps, and that the manager can take action to change perceptions of change from negative to positive.
• How supportive is your organization in encouraging risk-taking and change?	6. You can't do a quick-fix on culture. If you haven't got a supportive culture, then the patient may die before you can carry out the change operation. Willingness for change can only be built by painstaking investment of time, money and effort in creating an internal market for change, saturation levels of education and immersion in the real world of customers and pound notes.
	7. It is natural for people to resist change. By anticipating, identifying and welcoming resistance we convert raw objections into a powerhouse of energy for change. Rather than a hard sell on the benefit of change, we may do better to minimize sources of resistance. There are some useful tools and techniques to help.
• What is your personal leadership vision and does anyone else know about it?	8. It is a shared vision of the future which provides the pull-through for change. The more time we spend inventing 'what if' scenarios and visualizing new possibilities, the more we start to move away from the predictable past. You can't build a shared

Figure 11.1   Summary of key messages and challenges

vision in the isolation of your office. In times of rapid change the role of CEO as visionary leader is vital, both in articulating, communicating and living the vision and in constantly alerting the management team to new challenges, threats and alternative worldviews.

9. If what you've got is OK, then why change? Change won't happen unless there is widely acknowledged dissatisfaction with the status quo. This means positively encouraging open debate and the expression of dissonant views, rebels and mavericks who see that the emperor has no clothes. You may have to destabilize and engineer a crisis to get movement.

- How are you spreading the message?

10. Communications are the antidote to the uncertainty of change. The manager must overdose, communicate like crazy. Lack of communication is the most frequently cited reason for the failure of change programmes. Top-down change doesn't work. You need bottom-up and early involvement. The right kind of communication mechanisms, many simultaneous mechanisms.

11. Time and timing of change is crucial. It always takes longer than you think.

Figure 11.1–*contd.*

11.3 Becoming a change star

This chapter aims to translate the main themes of the book into a practical guide, which will help you plan for and implement any specific change you have in mind. Clearly, one important measure of the efficiency of the change process is the quality of the change itself, the new strategy, structure or process you are planning to put in place. Chapters 1 and 2 aimed to help you assess the appropriateness of your agenda for change in terms of its 'fit' with the environmental pressures facing you. But there are other important criteria for assessing the change process and these relate not so much to what you are going to do, as to the commitment and participation of key people, the human costs of changing and the time it takes to make change happen.

It is quite difficult to come up with a 1–10 list of doing change, because the change process is so messy. One has to do a lot of

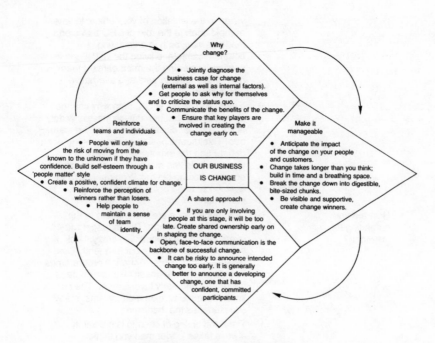

Figure 11.2 The change star

things at the same time and be prepared to revisit and repeat
ground covered earlier. While a step-by-step approach is sensible, it
pays to remember that the change will actually change as you go
along and also that there will be many feedback loops in the
process, which make it dangerous to be too simplistic or to plan too
much detail in advance.

Take, for example, the 'change' star model (Figure 11.2). The
model arose from practical work in ICL in the 1980s, and was
invented to help create a vocabulary which managers could use in
thinking through a change. The change star is a useful summary of
many of the pointers we have considered in this book, but it has
distinct drawbacks as a framework for planning a specific change.
The first is, where to start? The obvious place would be at the top of
the change star in diagnosing and communicating the need for
change. However, if we wait to involve people until, moving
clockwise, we get to 6 o'clock on the change star, then it will be too
late. Open communications are the bedrock of change at any stage
of the change process. Similarly, starting with 'why' the change is
entirely logical, but in the process of identifying resistance and
'making it manageable' you may come to the conclusion that the

costs of change outweigh any potential benefits and that you shouldn't therefore do it at all.

Most important of all, it is clear that implementing a specific change exists on a different timescale from creating the organizational culture which is conducive to change. In trying to use the change star to help handle a one-off change, even the best of managers will find that he or she cannot build overnight that receptive climate of trust, positive reinforcement and participation which will reinforce teams and individuals and create willingness for change.

Having said this, many managers have found the change star a good guide on their journey of change. Let's consider each 'pointer' in turn.

11.3.1 Why change?

This 'pointer' reminds us that change is prompted by external as well as internal factors, and that this must be made clear by explaining the business case for change, encouraging everyone to ask 'why' for themselves and constantly identifying problems and finding better solutions. The reasons for change and the possible advantages are not always as obvious as they may seem to top management and need to be communicated over and over again. To win active commitment, ensure that as many of the key players as possible are in the change early on, before it becomes a *fait accompli*.

11.3.2 Make it manageable

Even when there is dissatisfaction with the status quo and a clear and shared picture of what is needed, the change may not happen. It may be too big for anyone to handle – breaking it down into manageable bits is therefore essential. The first step is to anticipate the impact of change on individuals, teams and customers: the knock-on effects may be substantial. Change takes longer than you think. The preparation for change involves mental adjustment, thorough training, provision of tools and the introduction of new processes. Creating a breathing space during a change allows time for these preparations and gives you a chance to review, take stock and change the change as it goes along. You can also make a change more manageable by dividing it into bite-sized chunks: eat your elephant a bite at a time! This helps on two counts: first, realistic goals can be successfully achieved (this gives the change credibility and gives the participants confidence); and second, getting started towards a new vision may be difficult. Short, intermediate goals make it easier to take the first step and result in more change winners.

11.3.3   Share the change

Shared ownership means that it is everyone's change, not just yours, comfort is increased, resistance minimized. Open communication means talking about change every step of the way, allowing people to express their doubts and being prepared to build their input into how change is shaped.

11.3.4   Reinforce teams and individuals

Your colleagues will feel more willing to accept change if they have confidence in themselves and a high degree of self-esteem. This means creating a learning environment, a positive attitude towards change which fosters risk-taking and experimentation. This can be done through 'positive reinforcement', giving rewards, highlighting success stories, reassuring people, celebrating achievement and giving personal attention and counselling.

11.4   A process for leading change

Having talked about the drawbacks of a simple step-by-step approach, such an approach is still a great deal better than nothing at all. At least it provides a basis for thinking through and planning for problems in advance. In knitting together the threads of this book, stemming from our original model of the elements of a change process, we suggest a process chart (Figure 11.3), which can be used to help you manage both change in general and also any specific change you may be contemplating.

11.4.1   Sensitize via change culture

Change means opportunity as well as threat. Whether people see it in this light depends on the internal market or climate for change. If you have the willingness for change in the first place, then you won't be pushing a snowball uphill every time you try to change something in the organization. That is why so much of the essence of change lies around long-term work on internal attitudes and

Essential pre-work *Sensitize via change culture*

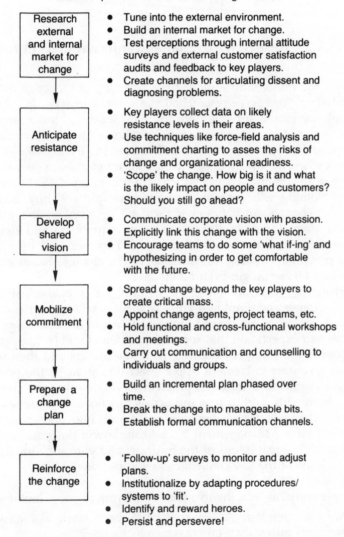

Research external and internal market for change	• Tune into the external environment. • Build an internal market for change. • Test perceptions through internal attitude surveys and external customer satisfaction audits and feedback to key players. • Create channels for articulating dissent and diagnosing problems.
Anticipate resistance	• Key players collect data on likely resistance levels in their areas. • Use techniques like force-field analysis and commitment charting to asses the risks of change and organizational readiness. • 'Scope' the change. How big is it and what is the likely impact on people and customers? Should you still go ahead?
Develop shared vision	• Communicate corporate vision with passion. • Explicitly link this change with the vision. • Encourage teams to do some 'what if-ing' and hypothesizing in order to get comfortable with the future.
Mobilize commitment	• Spread change beyond the key players to create critical mass. • Appoint change agents, project teams, etc. • Hold functional and cross-functional workshops and meetings. • Carry out communication and counselling to individuals and groups.
Prepare a change plan	• Build an incremental plan phased over time. • Break the change into manageable bits. • Establish formal communication channels.
Reinforce the change	• 'Follow-up' surveys to monitor and adjust plans. • Institutionalize by adapting procedures/ systems to 'fit'. • Identify and reward heroes. • Persist and persevere!

Figure 11.3 A process for leading change

behaviour, achieved through education, changing managerial mind sets, immersing employees in the customers' perspective, vision building, surfacing dissatisfaction, constant and open communications.

11.4.2 Research external and internal market for change

To you, the reasons for – indeed the necessity of – change may be crystal clear. You have researched the external market for change through customer surveys and through scanning the economic, social and technical environment. You know that it is a case of change or die. This is not enough. If you start to try to make change happen when the business case is in your mind alone, you will find that you are pulling a lever which is not connected to the engine room. Nothing will happen. Generally, people will buy into the need for change much better if they are involved at the earliest possible stage, in jointly diagnosing business problems and identifying for themselves the reasons for change. This means that you have to be prepared to make adjustments to the change, based on the input and ideas you get from others.

Fortunately, there are lots of mechanisms which enable you to do this. Customer and employee attitude surveys will bring dissatisfaction and pressures for change to the surface and in themselves start to create an expectation that something different will be happening. By sharing the emergent findings with key players and then wider groups you start to create a ripple effect, the stone in the pond of change. Formal and informal problem-solving workshops and sessions, both with work teams and across functional boundaries, will provide channels for challenging the status quo and expressing dissident views. Management by walkabout will put you in closer touch with the real issues of the business and your individuals and teams. Some of the key challenges to you personally are:

- How early can you involve the key players in your thinking?
- Are you confident enough to ask groups to work on issues and problems rather than on *fait accompli* changes?
- Do you really listen to what customers are telling you?
- How strong is the external justification, the 'business case', for making this change?
- Where is the legitimacy for doing so (data on customer or employee dissatisfaction, environmental trends)?

- How are you encouraging a groundswell of feeling within the organization which will give you the critical mass for change?

11.4.3 Anticipating resistance

Part of building the internal market for change is anticipating the source and strength of resistance. If resistance is sky high then there may be very little point in trying to sell change into such a tough market. The alternatives may be to soften the change by reducing levels of resistance, or even to offer a different change product which may be more acceptable. We've already talked about the technique of force-field analysis, commitment charting and assessing organization readiness. The advantage of these tools is that they give you a framework for working with your management team or key players in monitoring resistance further down the organization. Similarly, if you have already appointed change agents, mini-leaders or project teams to help implement change, then they can also do 'dipstick' checks of resistance levels.

'Scoping' the change in this way will allow you to assess the cost/benefit equation of change and turn back before it is too late. For example, if a great many staff are affected by the change, if it affects security of employment, if the team identity, working environment and job responsibilities are at risk, then it is probably a big change. Similarly, if the change affects the continuity of the sales relationship with key customers, is going to precipitate retaliation by competitors or provoke negative press comment, then it begins to look like a substantial change.

At this stage, having researched the external and internal market for change and involved your key players in diagnosing the need for change and likely levels of resistance, you are in a position to consolidate and feed back the results to a wider group. The 'strawman' becomes a 'tinman' as the ripple effect of change spreads out.

11.4.4 Develop shared vision

Creating a vision of the future is part of the longer-term culture-building activity, but it is also an immediate factor in the process of implementing a specific change. As the change equation has illustrated, reinforcing the desirability of the future is an important part of ensuring that the benefit of change exceeds the costs. This means that for any organization or strategic change to make sense, the corporate vision needs to be strongly rearticulated, and any communications need to demonstrate explicitly that the proposed change is consistent with stated vision and values.

As the circle of people who are involved in the change spreads out, so envisaging the future becomes critical to mobilizing commitment. At this point it is very useful to bring into team workshops, meetings and presentations some of the 'what if' techniques described in Chapter 7 so that people can become comfortable with the idea of the future. Some key challenges to you at this stage in the process are:

- What is your vision of the future and is anyone else as committed to it as you are?
- How convinced are you that the change you're envisaging is consistent with your established vision and values?
- How can you articulate and communicate the vision anew?
- How can you explicitly link this change to the vision?

11.4.5   Mobilize commitment to change

Before putting together a plan for the 'roll out' of the change it pays to make sure that involvement so far has converted a few key players into a critical mass for change. Yet again this means communicating like crazy, checking and rechecking, understanding and consulting. Feedback allows the realignment of the change, open communications provide the opportunity for questions and answers.

There are some simple rules of thumb. Someone needs to be given the task of spreading the change: team leaders, change agents, facilitators or project groups. The process of actually understanding and gaining commitment, both for key players and as the targeted group gets larger, should involve some element of group, then individual, then group communications. This way, the team in question can get a general and consistent overview of the change and can be asked to go away and think about their individual problems and concerns, to be revisited on an appointed day. This provides the opportunity to counsel individuals who are at risk, clear up misunderstandings and respond to individual issues. A final group meeting then reseals the intent and the way forward.

It always pays to allow people time to think and to have lots of small pieces of communication rather than one 'big bang' announcement. Commitment workshops can help spread the message and prepare affected groups. Open meetings of large numbers can be productive, providing there is the opportunity for questions and answers in smaller 'break-out' groups. Challenges to you at this point include:

- Do you think you have sufficient people on board with change to provide 'critical mass'?
- Who are the people who will 'seed' and spread the change process on your behalf?
- Where are you in converting your change from a 'strawman' to a 'tinman' to an 'ironman'?
- How prepared are you, even at this stage, to accept constant feedback, keep rechecking understanding and modify the change plan in the light of new data?

11.4.6 Preparing a change plan

It may well have taken many weeks and months to get to this stage in the change process, but it will be time well spent. Almost finally, as change becomes a developing reality, it will be essential to prepare a phased schedule which allows those concerned to manage the process incrementally. A realistic schedule will probably be twice as long as you first thought; be prepared to review the process at each stage. Lead-times will need to be built in for counselling, for logistics like getting computers and office equipment in place, for allowing project teams investigating the detailed 'how' of change to report back. If possible, pace the change so that there are some breaks or 'bubbles' of time when people have the breathing space to catch up with themselves and with the requirement to 'keep the shop open' while change is taking place. You will need formal communication channels in place which detail exactly who will say what to whom, how and when, so that the message is clear and consistent and no one is left out. As usual, two-way, face-to-face communications are always better than using the telephone, letter or noticeboard. Perhaps managers worry too much about the need for a mass top-down announcement at the same minute of the day to everyone. Given the logistics of manning telephones, drawing the salesforce in from the field, trying not to forget people who are on holiday, it is well nigh impossible. If the idea of the change has been around for some time, it may well also be unnecessary. Key challenges to you include:

- Is the timescale of change realistic?

- How can you break a large change into small manageable bits?
- What face-to-face communication channels have you put in place?
- What is the 'safety net' of support and counselling?
- Have you built in 'transitional time' to allow space for the change to evolve?

Your plan for change will probably look much more like a critical path flowchart than a change star, but you might like to use Figure 11.4 to check that you are on the right lines.

11.4.7   Reinforce the change

As the roll-out of change is implemented, many managers may be ready to breathe a deep sign of relief, congratulate themselves on a job well done and collapse in a heap. No such luck. Making change stick means that there is still vital work to be done in institutionalizing and 'refreezing' to ensure that the environment remains supportive to the change and people don't revert to their pre-change behaviours. Having used the approach of selling change into the internal market, we need to follow up and take some measures of external and internal client satisfaction. The pay-offs will be several: first, in enabling us to monitor and adjust tactics, second, in reaffirming the continuity of the change, third, in flagging up 'best practice' which can then spread to revitalize other parts of the organization.

Inevitably, there will be issues of job redefinition and reallocation

---

1. What are the major change issues to be managed (i.e. resistance levels, break-up of teams, winners and loser, timing, training)?

-
-
-
-
-
-

Figure 11.4   Planning for change

2. What does your step-by-step, phased flowchart of 'roll-out' look like?

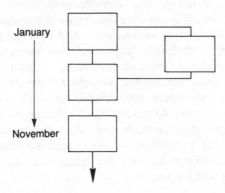

3. Does your plan adequately cover the issues you raised in Point 1 and the 'pointers' of the change star?

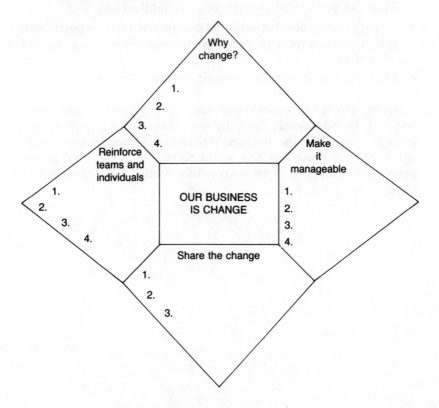

Figure 11.4–*contd.*

of resources as the dust settles and the implications of the change become clearer. Training and development needs are likely to emerge. In addition, it is possible that existing management systems and practices will need to be 'tweaked' and perhaps new processes put in place. It is obviously important that every aspect – from recruitment procedures, through induction, training, appraisal and career development – are aligned to reinforce the change.

We need to create some very visible 'heroes' from among the ranks of those who are role modelling the change successfully. They should be acknowledged publicly and, of course, rewarded. And we shouldn't wait for perfection – even small successes should be rewarded quickly to provide positive reinforcement. A quick check of the following will help you:

- What kind of validation process/follow-up survey have you put in place?
- How can you spread best practice around the company?
- Are there any obvious areas where aspects of the operational, information, reward or appraisal systems are working against your change?
- How can you identify and reward heroes?

Finally, change is a continuous and exciting journey with some rest periods and rewards along the way. However, it is unlikely that we will ever reach the planned destination before things change again. Most definitely in this world there will be no final arrival point. One change may be successfully rooted, but others are to come.

Further reading

If you:

- want to know what other people have thought about change,
- are interested in how different companies and nations tackle the issue of change,
- have a professional interest in managing change,
- simply want to know more,

then you could try reading some of the books described below. This list is by no means exhaustive but it is a good place to start.

Asimov, Isaac, *Foundation*, Grafton Books, London, 1962.

Bartlett, Christopher and Ghoshal Sumantra, *Managing Across Borders: The transnational solution*, Business Books, Random House Group, 1992.

Beckhard, Richard and Harris, Reuben T., *Organizational Transitions*, Addison-Wesley, Wokingham, 1987.

Belbin, R. M., *Management Teams: Why they succeed or fail*, Heinemann, London, 1981.

Deal, Terrence E. and Kennedy, Allen A., *Corporate Cultures: Rites and rituals of corporate life*, Penguin Books, London, 1988.

de Bono, Edward, *Serious Creativity*, Harper-Collins, London, 1992.

Gorbachev, Mikhail, *Perestroika*, Fontana/Collins, London, 1987.

Greiner, Larry E., 'Evolution and Revolution as Organizations Grow', *HBR* reprint No. 72407, July/August 72, 1972.

Handy, Charles, *The Age of Unreason*, Arrow Books, London, 1990.

Hart, Gary, *The Second Russian Revolution*, Hodder & Stoughton, London, 1991.

Holmes, Thomas and Rahe, Richard, 'The social readjustment rating scale', *Journal of Psychosomatic Research*, Volume 2, No. 2, 1967.

James, Kim and Arroba, Tanya, *Pressure at Work: A survival guide for managers*, 2nd edition, McGraw-Hill, Maidenhead, 1992.

Kanter, Rosabeth Moss, *The Change Masters: Corporate entrepreneurs at work*, Unwin, London, 1985.

Kidder, Tracy, *Soul of a New Machine*, Penguin Books, London, 1987.

KPMG Career Consultancy Services Pamphlet, *Partners: Coping with redundancy*, November 1992.

Majaro, Simon, *Managing Ideas for Profit – The Creative Gap*, McGraw-Hill, Maidenhead, 1992.

Murray Parkes, Colin, *Bereavement: Studies of grief in adult life*, Pelican Books, London, 1975.

Pascale, Richard Tanner and Athos, Anthony G., *The Art of Japanese Management*, Penguin Books, London, 1982.

Plant, Roger, *Managing Change and Making it Stick*, Fontana, London, 1987.

Prahalad, C. K. and Doz, Yves, *The Multi-National Mission*, Collier Macmillan, London, 1987.

Roberts, Wess, *Leadership Secrets of Attila the Hun*, Bantam Books, London, 1990.

Roddick, Anita, *Body & Soul*, Ebury Press, London, 1991.

Schein, Edgar H., 'How can organizations learn faster? The challenge of entering the green room', *Sloan Management Review Reprint Series*, Volume 34, No. 2, Reprint 3428, Winter 1993.

Watzlawick, P., Weakland, J. and Fisch, R., *Change, Principles of Problem Formulation and Problem Resolution*, Norton Inc., New York, 1974.

Index

199